EVIDENCE SCENE

Members of Missouri K-9 Search and Rescue met investigators on the gravel road that led to John Robinson's farm, outside La Cygne, Kansas. The K-9 teams went in first, about 9:00 A.M. The handlers had their dogs sniff around the trailer before crime scene investigators began processing the trailer's interior.

"It looked like it was going to be a disappointment," said Sergeant Rick Roth of Lenexa Police Department. "The inside was a wreck, and the only item of significance that I could see initially was a Big Boy box matching the ones that [one of the missing women] had brought from Michigan."

The K-9 teams worked east to a collapsed building and a nearby concrete foundation, then south to the pond near the back of the property. While detectives combed other areas, Overland Park's five-member underwater team began a hand search of the snake-infested pond, looking for bodies, weapons, clothes or anything else that might point to foul play. It was a hot, humid day. The chiggers were in legions.

During the lunch break, K-9 handler Petra Stephens approached Roth and asked if he could have someone move some barrels away from a small shed. One of her Border Collies had shown some interest.

Roth threw a few items out of the way and began rocking one of the yellow drums from side to side as he pulled it backwards. Hitting an area of grass and bushes, he laid the barrel on its side, rolled it to a clearing and stood it back up. That's when he saw it: a single bead of reddish liquid that rolled from the edge of the lid down the side of the barrel.

"Is that blood?" someone asked.

The first body had been found. It was far from the last. . . .

SLAVE MASTER

SUE WILTZ

with Maurice Godwin, Ph.D.

PINNACLE BOOKS
Kensington Publishing Corp.
http://www.kensingtonbooks.com

ACKNOWLEDGMENTS

Many people made this book possible.

First and foremost, my deepest gratitude goes to Sergeant Rick Roth, who spent countless hours recalling details from the Robinson police probe, generously offering his personal and professional insights with a wry sense of humor and an unfaltering commitment to accuracy.

I am likewise indebted to many others in the law enforcement community who so kindly gave of their time, talent and expertise: Johnson County district attorney Paul Morrison and Johnson County assistant district attorney Sara Welch, Overland Park sergeant Joe Reed, Overland Park detectives Greg Wilson, Bobbi Jo Hohnholt, Mike Jacobson and Scott Weiler, Lenexa sergeant Dave Brown, Lenexa detectives Jake Boyer, Brad Hill, Mike Lowther, Dawn Layman, Alan Beyer, Perry Meyer, Mike Bussell, Rick Dougan, and Dan Owsley, Liberty (Missouri) parole supervisor Stephen Haymes, Overland Park captain Keith O'Neal, Lenexa Police Chief Ellen Hanson, Lenexa captain John Meier and Cass County district attorney Chris Koster.

My sincerest appreciation goes to the Trouten family, Karen Moore, Vickie Neufeld, Suzanne and Debbie Lawrence, Sharon LaPrad, Carl Macan, Debbie Mahan, Peggy Breit, Jeff Roberts, Tony Rizzo, John Milburn, Lisa Carter, Gerald Hay, Terri Issa, Linda Carter, Shirley Fessler, Ron Keefover, Mike McLain, April Shepard and the many other wonderful people I met while reporting this book. I am obligated to still others who do not wish to be identified, particularly the defense source who provided me with access to certain police documents, lending this narrative some of its illuminating and previously unpublished details.

I also wish to recognize my agents, Jane Dystel and Miriam Goderich; my editor at Kensington, Michaela Hamilton, my friends and former colleagues at *People* magazine,

AUTHOR'S NOTE

The material in this book is drawn from personal interviews and recollections, police and court records, witness testimony and news reports, including *The Kansas City Star,* the *Olathe Daily News* and the Associated Press. Pseudonyms or first names were used for a few individuals on the periphery of this case, solely at the author's discretion. Lastly, no editorial promises were made or money offered in exchange for information.

Prologue

Detectives Jake Boyer and Greg Wilson had a surprise waiting for John E. Robinson Sr. back at the Lenexa, Kansas, police station shortly after his arrest on the morning of June 2, 2000. Escorting the shackled prisoner into a conference room, they instructed him to remain silent. "We are going to respect the fact that you have asked for your attorney," Wilson said. "But we want you to understand how much work we have done and how much we know about your activities."

On a table in the center of the conference room lay photographs of several women whom Robinson had recently met for sadomasochistic sex, including Vickie Neufeld and Jeanna Milliron. A second table held seven black binders, containing hundreds of pages from an exhaustive ten-week investigation. Taped to a bulletin board was a picture of Suzette Marie Trouten, her police case number scrawled beside it, grainy surveillance photos of Robinson and his wife, Nancy, and a hand-drawn map with directions to his rural Kansas farm.

Slowly and silently, the fifty-six-year-old prisoner—balding, pudgy and bespectacled—walked around the center table, pausing for several seconds to stare intently at each photo.

Returning to the police booking room, detectives removed his handcuffs and allowed him to phone his lawyer. Robinson explained to attorney Ron Wood that he'd been arrested on charges of aggravated sexual battery, blackmail and felony theft. Bond, he calmly added, had been set for $250,000.

Chapter 1

In February 2000, Suzette Marie Trouten was excited about the future. The twenty-seven-year-old nurse's aide recently had met a man on the Internet who offered her a job in Kansas caring for his diabetic, wheelchair-bound father. She told friends and family the job would last about a year and entail world travel, time off every three months and great benefits. But the best part, gushed the vivacious brunette, was that the $65,000 salary he promised would allow her to pay for the pricey training she needed to become a registered nurse.

Nursing was a dream that Suzette had nurtured since she was a young girl growing up in the small town of Newport, Michigan, the youngest of Harry and Carolyn Trouten's five children and every bit the baby of the boisterous, tight-knit family. She had always adored animals—riding at age two the family's pet bull—and it wouldn't be long before she became just as devoted to caring for the elderly and terminally ill.

Perhaps the trauma she endured in childhood made her particularly sensitive to the pain and suffering of others. When she was eleven, Suzette was raped by a member of a nearby boat club, her mother said. Roughly the same time, her parents separated and eventually divorced. Because of the assault and her parents' breakup, Suzette wound up spending nearly a year in the psychiatric unit at Monroe County Hospital.

Even after her release, Suzette kept trying to reunite her parents. One day, devastated by a teenage breakup of her own, she was talking to her mother when she pulled out a gun and shot herself in the stomach. The bullet caused no permanent

"When I called to check on her a little later that day, the woman's husband said she learned it like a pro," LaPrad recalled. "She was always willing and wanting to know more."

Suzette made about $10 an hour as a nurse's aide, which wasn't enough to save for nursing school *and* cover living expenses, including the $200 rent she paid for a room in the home of her friend John Stapleton. She began working two or three shifts a week as a cook at the local Big Boy restaurant, where her mother was the manager. By 1998, she had taken a lot of nursing prerequisite courses and saved enough for a nursing program at Monroe County Community College only to drop out after being hospitalized with an undiagnosed illness for several weeks. "She really wanted to get her degree," recalled her sister Dawn. "She wanted to be a nurse."

Suzette was disappointed at the setback, her mother said, but her daughter's spirits were once again buoyed when a wealthy businessman named John Robinson offered her the "dream job" in Kansas. She planned to work with him for a year, touring the world yet still saving money, then come home and finally finish her nursing degree. "She had been going part-time and working," Carolyn said. "This way, she thought she could save up some money and go straight through."

There was some confusion over how Suzette had met Robinson. She told LaPrad she had found the opportunity through the wife of a physician friend who ran a nationwide home-care business. She told her sister Kim Padilla that it had come through LaPrad. They wouldn't discover these discrepancies until later, however. What they knew in the fall of 1999 is that Suzette and Robinson had somehow connected through the Internet and were now exchanging e-mail and talking regularly on the phone.

Only Kim and close friends such as Lore Remington and Tami Taylor were aware that Suzette actually led a double life: she was secretly involved in what is known as BDSM—an umbrella term for sexual activities involving bondage and discipline, domination and submission, sadism and masochism.

versing daily in ICQ instant-messaging sessions on the Internet and quickly becoming the closest of friends. Lore later introduced her to Tami, another Gorean submissive, who lived in Ontario, and the three were in regular contact, chitchatting about their everyday lives as well as their sexual experiences with dominant male partners. Suzette, a bisexual, became intimate with both women, separately, when each visited Michigan and they participated in three-way BDSM sessions with different masters.

In 1999, Suzette had placed an ad on ALT.com, a Fetish/BDSM "personals" Web site that claims more than a million members. Calling herself "angelwithout," she indicated she was "looking for the right Master" and went on to describe herself in the following terms:

> I am a 27 year old female who has been in BDSM for the last 11 years. I was owned from 16 to a year ago. I am 5'6" long brown hair, dark brown eyes, olive skin tone. I have a good shape and is a total slave. I live in Lower Michigan close to Detroit. I enjoy bondage, spankings, whips, is some what of a pain slut. No scat, blood, animals, no children . . . this is hard limits that will not be testeddddddd!!!!!!

For Suzette, September 11, 1999, would prove to be a very unlucky day indeed. "Read your ad," wrote "John Rob," using the e-mail address midwestmaster@email.com. "Let's talk about the possibilities."

Within days—which was moving very fast even by the standards of BDSM—Suzette had agreed to become his slave, telling him all about herself ("I love to read, write, paint, horse back riding, walks, fishing. Enjoys the out doors greatly"), giving him passwords to her various e-mail accounts and laying the initial plans for her move to Kansas City. She signed many of her notes, "On bended knee, Suzette."

On September 17, 1999, Robinson sent Suzette an e-mail

She returned to Michigan both times saying how impressed she was with what she had seen. She said Robinson was a wealthy man, who had picked her up in an airport limousine, taken her to his mansion and treated her like a queen. She described meeting Robinson's wife, a younger woman with blond hair. She also said she had met "Papa John," Robinson's elderly father, "a crotchety old man," as she put it, and the young woman who had been his previous caretaker and was now an attorney. "She had so many details, it couldn't have been made up," Carolyn insisted.

Papa John owned several international companies, Suzette explained, but Robinson had been running them for his father, who wasn't well and was eager to step down and travel the world. One of Suzette's first trips after she got to Kansas would be to accompany both of them to Europe, taking care of Papa John while Robinson handled business in Switzerland and Belgium.

Robinson suggested Suzette apply for a passport and begin researching nursing programs overseas because she would probably have time to take some classes. Her mother remembered Suzette spending an entire afternoon on the Internet, looking up nursing programs in Belgium, and filling out the paperwork in Michigan for a passport. She never submitted the application because she was told she would need to apply through her new home in Kansas.

Robinson certainly seemed friendly and normal enough whenever he called Carolyn's house and asked to speak to her daughter. "He called here a lot and she would talk to him and tell me what he said," recalled her mother, who knew him well enough to say hello to after Suzette had moved home shortly before leaving Michigan. "One time, she said he had been working all day at the shelter—that everyone in his company goes to feed the poor. He seemed like a very nice man."

Carolyn admitted it was "fishy" that Robinson had agreed to pay Suzette such a large salary, but then she decided it wasn't so unusual considering she would be working long

of mixed emotions: excited and scared at the same time. She had never lived anywhere else. *It will be strange being in a place I don't know,* she thought to herself. *Everything here is so familiar*. She was just a big mama's girl, she realized, and it was going to be hard to be so far from home.

agreed to board them for her in a nearby kennel, Ridgeview Animal Hospital. "Strange being alone in my room," she wrote that day.

Over the next several days, she suffered through a cold, bouts of sleeplessness and the end of a heavy two-week menstrual period, which she referred to as her "vampire weeks" in conversations with Lore. She would be moody and anxious one day, happy and relaxed the next. "I came, I saw, I want to come home," she wrote on February 19 in an ICQ message to her sister Kim. "Am homesick."

Two days later, her spirits soared as Robinson told her they would be leaving on their first trip, a week from Monday. By this time, the plans had changed, however, and instead of Europe they would be driving to California to pick up a yacht Robinson had purchased recently and sailing from there to Hawaii. The new destination didn't seem to faze Suzette; she told friends she was eager to check out Thai restaurants in California. "I am excited about going," she wrote in her journal.

She wasn't really working just yet but settling in, she told her mom. Robinson was busy negotiating the sale of one of his companies and they would be leaving for California as soon as he was done. She did mention she was working on some sort of Web site, but Carolyn, who detested computers even then, never asked about the details.

Suzette was more candid with Lore, finally admitting that there was more to her move to Kansas City than the job. She acknowledged that not only was she going to take care of Robinson's elderly father but was also developing a Web site for him about a secret BDSM society called the International Council of Masters, and that he was one of its "elite" members. She also admitted very cryptically that she and the younger Robinson were engaging in sadomasochistic sex. "When she went to Kansas, it was for a job," Lore later said, "but she finally told me the truth. I said, 'You're involved with him, aren't you?' and she said yes. She didn't tell me [before] because she knew I'd be irate. You don't mix business with pleasure."

his permission—which infuriated him. Suzette also seemed to have decided by this point that she was going to keep her relationship with Robinson on a purely professional level. "Just don't fuck the boss," Lore had pleaded. "I won't baby. Will screw up a great thing if I do," Suzette answered. A little later, she wrote, apparently to placate her friend, "No I'm not doing him and him is boss you were talking about."

The next morning, March 1, Suzette logged on to her America Online account at 9:09 A.M. from the telephone line in her room at the Guesthouse Suites. While on the Internet that morning, she accessed her e-mail account at Hotmail.com in order to send and receive e-mail, signing off at 9:24 A.M. Before logging off, she also held an ICQ chat session with an Australian friend, who used the online nickname "ahsa." "We leave tomorrow," Suzette wrote. "Will be gone about 2 to 6 months . . . nothing like taking a vacation while working. Well sweets I have to run . . . am off to the farm this morning for a while . . . grins . . . love to both of you baby."

The "farm" was Robinson's 16.5-acre property, located about an hour south of Kansas City in rural Linn County, which he had bought in May 1994. Though it contained nothing more than a ramshackle trailer, an old barn and a fishing pond, it was his pride and joy.

On the morning of March 2, Lore received an e-mail from Suzette, writing now from her Hotmail e-mail account instead of from her usual ICQ chat. "By the time you get this I [*sic*] off," it said. "My computer crashed yesterday and it took hours to get it working. You would laugh, station wagon full, the dogs in the back and off we go on the adventure of a lifetime . . . sees ya . . . suz."

At first, Lore didn't doubt the authenticity of the e-mail and sent her friend a reply, telling her to "have a blast" on the trip. She also mentioned she had told her master "to take a fucking leap" when he insisted he would be the only one to decide when she could get her nipples pierced. She was through with him, she told Suzette.

they would be on their way to a Dominant/submissive relationship. "I warn you up front I am a very demanding
MASTER," he wrote. "If I accept you, you will be my slave
and you will understand your place is at my feet on your
knees. There is no quarter given." JT said his first rule was
daily communication and he ordered Lore to e-mail him
every day before 9 A.M. CST.

Lore's suspicions grew as she noted that JT also spelled
master in all capital letters. She continued e-mailing him as
well as whoever was using her friend's Hotmail account. She
asked "Suzette" what she knew about JT, adding that her ex-
master was furious with her and she was now thinking of
"playing" with some other Doms.

Suzette was obviously miffed when she purportedly wrote
back on March 7. "Lore; you know sometimes I would like to
strangle the fuck out of you," she wrote. "I would not have
even mentioned this guy if I tought [*sic*] he would be bad for
you." She went on to say she thought Lore could use a little
"quality dominance" in her life and she shouldn't screw
things up with JT by telling him she needed to play with other
dominants. "I have been through the same bull shit you have,
bad scenes, bad Doms who only wanted to hurt me, bad shit
and you know how it bothers me," she wrote. "I hoipe [*sic*]
this is my knight in shining armour, sems [*sic*] to be, feels that
way, and I'm going to keep him as happy as any slut could
possibly keep him." She also told Lore to relax and stop always looking for the down side. "Look for the potential, the
hope, the real MASTER," she wrote. "I'm telling you, this
MASTER can have the pick of the litter, be flattered he is
thinking seriously about you!!!" Reminding Lore that she
didn't have her computer and was stopping where she could,
she said she would monitor her progress. Telling her to be
happy, Suzette signed off with "Love ya lots."

Over the next few days, Lore learned from JT that his full
name was "James R. Turner," or "Jim Turner," and he was a
vice president of human resources at a large company in the

and upset," she later said. "None of the questions I was asking were being answered. The hints and little things I was sending weren't being responded to, but I was getting phone calls from [JT] addressing them. The more questions I asked, the more the e-mails were getting angrier and had a don't-ask attitude. Then my questions were not being answered by the e-mail Suzette. I received one more around [March] twentieth and that was it."

By now Lore had confided in Tami, showing her the e-mails she'd received and telling her how worried she was for Suzette's safety. After discussing what to do, the two women came up with a plan. Lore e-mailed "Suzette," asking her if her new master had any single friends for Tami. "Does Tami think I am the clearing house for MASTERS?" joked "Suzette." She suggested that Lore send Tami's e-mail address to JT, who knew a lot of people in the lifestyle. JT, in turn, told Lore to have Tami contact a new master at another e-mail address, preipo@usa.net.

Tami sent a quick note to the address she'd been given, telling him she knew nothing about him other than the fact that he was seeking a new sub/slave. She told him she was divorced, with no children, and included a photo of herself. "Love those tits, oh you have really made my head swim," came the reply from a man calling himself "T" on March 16. "I am a tit person, I just love my slave to have nice large, firm tits just like yours." He outlined his needs, telling her that he was a total "MASTER" who wanted a long-term, 24/7 relationship. "What I require of my slave is 'everything,'" he wrote. "I want total obedience, total honesty and complete submission. I will use you, but I will also cherish you, care for you and love you. Now you ask me whatever questions you want and let's get on with beginning to develop a good solid, strong D/s relationship."

Within a few days, T, who also called himself "Tom," or "Thomas Anthony Thomas" was phoning Tami, leaving messages on her voice mail and urging her to come to Kansas City for a visit. While "T" wouldn't send her a picture of himself,

seem at all upset by the idea that her daughter had not taken the job. He had gone to great lengths—investing a lot of time and money on her trips out there—to be so nonchalant.

Shortly after Carolyn spoke to Robinson, several members of her family began to receive on March 21 e-mail from someone purporting to be Suzette:

> Well the wandering suz finally decided to drop everyone a note and say howdy. sorry no e-mail up until now . . . no excuses just lazy. Peka, Hari [*sic*] and I are fine, they travel really well. I'm in California and getting rested up for sailing . . . excited, what a opportunity. Promised Mom I would send her a doll from every country we go . . . John Edge has been trying to contact me and I told him to please leave me alone. He won't listen and sent me a threat about "finding me." don't worry about me, I'm a big girl . . . bigger than I should be, Love to all suz.

Marshella and her husband, Don, received another e-mail a few days later from "Suzette."

> By the time you get this we will be off. I have written mom and dad each a letter so mom can quit worrying. Will not be on line for some time, but will keep all posted on the trip every chance I get. I'm excited, Peka and Harri [*sic*] have taken to boat life like they were born for it. At first I thought they would start their wandering and fall off, but no problems. Well aloha . . . I love you guys. Suz.

Suzette was a terrible writer, but her family was certain she knew how to spell the names of her beloved dogs. They also thought she was crazy about John Edge and now she was telling them—uncharacteristically—she wanted him to leave her alone. The idea of Suzette on a boat didn't sit right with

Chapter 3

Overland Park police officer Warren Neff was working the evening shift on Saturday, March 25, when he took the fateful call from Suzette's sister Dawn, then living in Florida. Dawn tearfully explained the situation: her baby sister had obtained a job with a Kansas City businessman, only to disappear after spending a few weeks in a local hotel. She told him what her family and Suzette's friends knew and gave him phone numbers for her hotel and purported employer, John Robinson.

The name meant nothing to Neff. But to his supervisors, Lieutenant Dan Minteer and Sergeant Marty Ingram, who had investigated Robinson in the 1980s, it held great significance. Late Sunday evening, Minteer sent an e-mail about Suzette to Sergeant Joe Reed, who was in charge of detectives investigating crimes against persons. "I'd give this one close look," Minteer wrote Reed, prophetically entitling his note, "Strange Missing Person Case." "We still have some missing women on the books who had contact with [Robinson]."

Reed wasted no time when he got in on Monday morning. The likable, mustachioed sergeant loved his job. He had hired on with Overland Park fresh out of Central Missouri State University, where he majored in criminal justice. He'd worked a lot of cases in his twenty-two years on the force—burglaries, thefts and, ultimately, crimes against persons. His experience and instincts told him the Robinson case was going to be big. "I think we all recognized that right up front," he said. "We could have a serial killer on our hands."

and offering Overland Park's assistance. The two men were acquainted from having attended several of the same training seminars and having once worked the same murder investigation. Their departments—and their detectives—enjoyed a spirited rivalry as they policed adjacent upper-middle-class communities in the same county. The chief difference: Overland Park, with about 165,000 residents and 214 sworn police officers, was roughly three times the size of Lenexa.

Knowing that Overland Park was already familiar with Robinson's background, Roth decided to accept Reed's offer to commit Wilson and another of his detectives, Scott Weiler, to the investigation. (Hohnholt was finishing up another assignment.) While Weiler would return to his unit after three weeks to help with surveillance, Wilson would spend the next four months working out of the Lenexa detectives' conference room. Ultimately, Overland Park would play a major role as events unfolded.

Like Reed, Roth had spent his career in law enforcement. In 1974, he joined the Kansas City, Missouri, Police Department as a dispatcher, where he had met his good friend and future boss, Captain John Meier. Three years later, he had transferred to Lenexa, where he became a patrolman in 1979 and a sergeant in 1984, moving to investigations in 1997. A tall, dark and distinguished father of three grown sons and grandfather of two grandsons, Roth was about to become the immediate supervisor on the largest police probe in state history. Meanwhile, his twenty-five-year marriage to his high school sweetheart was starting to fall apart.

Roth immediately picked Dave Brown as the lead investigator. Experienced, organized and smart, the boyishly handsome detective was the perfect choice. But even as Roth talked to Brown, he realized the case might require even more than one crackerjack detective could handle. Returning to the training room, where a swearing in of new officers was about to begin, he pulled out Jake Boyer. A twenty-four-year police veteran, he was Roth's best "street" detective and brilliant at

est thing to a serial killer that Kansas City had ever seen, taking his victims to ATMs and draining their bank accounts before killing them. Even though the bodies were never found, the young prosecutor managed to win a conviction against Grissom after a four-week trial in 1990 that focused on an abundance of circumstantial and physical evidence. The landmark case attracted widespread media attention and prompted an ex-FBI agent to write the book, *Suddenly Gone*.

Five years after Grissom, Morrison prosecuted the equally bizarre case of Debora Green, the wealthy physician who had tried to poison her husband slowly and ultimately set her house on fire, killing two of her three children. Facing the death penalty, which had been reinstated in Kansas in 1994, Green ultimately pleaded guilty in exchange for life in prison. Like Grissom, she became the subject of many news articles and TV shows, as well as the mesmerizing bestseller *Bitter Harvest,* by well-known true crime writer Ann Rule.

Tall and lean with his thick mustache, chiseled features and subtle drawl, Morrison never sought publicity yet always seemed at ease in the spotlight. Born in Dodge City, Kansas, he hailed from a blue-collar family full of railroad workers and farmers. Growing up in tiny communities such as Plainville and Hays, he attended high school in Kansas City, Kansas, where he loved and excelled at debate. He and his brother were also into their Mustangs and motorcycles. "It was kind of a weird deal," he later said. "I was half debater, half gearhead. My dad used to tell me, 'You've got to figure out what you want to do.'"

He almost became a bricklayer. Dropping out of college for a year, he worked as a hod carrier—someone who assists a bricklayer in transporting loads of bricks and mortar—for a big construction company. "I tried really hard to get a bricklayer apprenticeship, but I didn't get my union card and instead got laid off," he recalled. "I always tell people that if I would have gotten that card, I'd be building chimneys around here somewhere."

Instead, he became the first male in his family to graduate

his wife had since left the news business and launched her own PR firm. "With Debora Green, it was a little tense. She'd be under pressure to get something and a lot of people didn't understand. When [Green] was arrested, channel 41 got the scoop. Turned out a cop had leaked the story. Well, my wife would not speak to me."

Before John Robinson, Morrison figured he'd probably already prosecuted his most sensational cases. "When Richard Grissom was done in 1990, I remember telling people, 'Gosh, it's too bad it came so early in my career. Everything's downhill from here—in terms of the really interesting and bizarre stuff,'" Morrison said. "Then five years later, along comes Debora Green. I think what it all means is that I am never ceased to be amazed by some of the things that people do."

To help with the Robinson case, Morrison called on ADA Sara Welch, one of his most experienced and skilled assistant district attorneys, who had just returned to work after major back surgery. Because she had been out for six weeks, all of her cases had been assigned to other attorneys and her calendar was clear for a big project. Morrison gave her the scoop and asked if she could go to Lenexa the following day to attend a police meeting on the subject. "This could be a huge deal or it might be a routine missing person case," Welch remembered him saying. "But women who associate with John Robinson seem to disappear."

Welch had grown up in the tiny town of Halstead, Kansas (the setting for the 1955 Academy Award–nominated movie *Picnic*) before spending nearly eight years as a cop in the Kansas City and Denver suburbs. She had worked the street and done a stint in undercover narcotics when, without much consideration or forethought, she applied and was accepted to the law school at the University of Colorado in Boulder. "I distinctly remember driving to my first law school final in December of 1985 and thinking, 'What in the hell am I

assigned Brown as the main contact for the Trouten family and the one who would investigate Suzette's association with Robinson. Boyer would have the pleasure of handling Lore Remington and Tami Taylor, the Canadian women. Brad Hill, a former marine who was on light-duty status because of a recent knee surgery, would immediately hit the phones to try and locate Suzette's dogs and any storage lockers where her belongings might be found.

The investigators agreed they should seal room 216 at the Guesthouse Suites and call in the Johnson County Crime Lab to process the scene. At Brown's suggestion, they wisely decided to put Robinson under surveillance and begin going through his trash. The responsibility of "trashing" went to Detective Dan Owsley, one of the department's two narcotics detectives who had experience collecting and retrieving evidence from suspects' garbage. Lenexa's Directed Patrol Unit, under Sergeant John Browning, was recruited to begin surveillance. Divided into two shifts, with detectives supplementing the officers, they would track Robinson's every move.

Roth was sitting at the conference table in investigations with his detectives that Tuesday morning when Sara walked in. "I still remember she was wearing a long black dress and she was walking with a cane!" Roth said. "Turns out she was wearing some sort of brace because of her recent back surgery and was in some pain. She was in such shape that she couldn't sit down during the meeting but instead leaned against the wall."

Up to that point, Roth had never worked with Welch, but he had heard she was highly regarded and also tough and tenacious—particularly in cases involving animal abuse. "She would drop anything to go after someone who was abusing [an animal]," Roth said. Welch only knew about the sergeant from what she had heard from his troops. "I had heard he was a real 'hard-ass,' never smiled, real aloof, all business, no joking around," she remembered. "I was intimidated by him and was very deferential to him when we first met."

Morrison, who joined the group a few minutes later, had

Chapter 4

From what the detectives knew going into the investigation, the balding fifty-six-year-old "businessman" didn't live in a mansion, as he had apparently claimed to Suzette Trouten. Instead, he resided in an immaculate but very modest gray-and-white trailer on Monterey Lane in a 486-unit mobile-home community called Santa Barbara Estates, located in the less affluent suburb of Olathe, just south of Lenexa and west of Overland Park.

Surveillance began on March 29, 2000. Browning and three of his officers watched as Robinson puttered around his trailer park all morning but never left. The afternoon shift was a different story. Detective Alan Beyer was just joining Officer Dustin Frackowiak around 2:00 P.M. when Robinson, driving his white Dodge Ram pickup, exited Santa Barbara Estates. They tailed him as he got on I-35 heading south, excitedly radioing the news back to headquarters. It wasn't long before he exited I-35 onto 169 Highway that their radios were all but worthless. They had reached an area so rural that soon their cell phones gave out, too.

Some of the detectives who had jumped in their cars to follow Beyer and Frackowiak could hear bits and pieces of radio traffic. Once in a while, they could make phone contact. Roth and Boyer were just plain lost. One officer stopped in the tiny hamlet of Paola, Kansas, and used a pay phone to call the Lenexa dispatcher, who in turn was able to reach the detectives and tell them where to turn. "We just kept driving," Roth remembered. "Once in a while, we'd hear someone on the radio

unfamiliar and shocked by the mechanics of BDSM, asked her to forward any correspondence she received. She agreed.

The next morning, March 30, Roth sent Detective Dawn Layman on a mission that defense lawyers would object to later. She returned to Robinson's property, which she would learn from records was a 16.5-acre parcel in Linn County. Parking in the driveway, she began taking photos of the trailer, a nearby shed and two rather beat-up–looking pickup trucks: a yellow Toyota and a red 1986 Ford. The windows on the trailer were covered with sheets of newspaper or black plastic; Layman got the impression it was vacant. There was also an odd assortment of junk in a heap next to the shed. One photo she took that morning revealed a lawn mower, an outboard motor and several barrels, including two yellow eighty-five-gallon metal drums. Of course, Layman had no clue at the time that she'd just captured a crime scene on film. "It was a little spooky," recalled the petite, athletic woman with short brown hair, who had been promoted to detective about three months before. "I wanted to get in and out of there as quickly as possible."

Records from the Linn County Assessor's Office listed Robinson as the owner of the parcel and affiliated with another company called Hydro-Gro, Inc., in Kansas City, Missouri. When Layman checked, she found that the address actually belonged to Accent Insurance, located in a small strip mall just south of I-470. Similarly, when Detective Perry Meyer ran a check on the address for Specialty Publications, which Robinson had used when he paid for Suzette's room at the Guesthouse Suites, he found three businesses: Home Equity and Personal Loans, Mail Plus and 1-Hour Photo. On the surface at least, it appeared that Robinson's businesses were phony.

On March 31, Brown received a call from Carolyn Trouten, whom he'd interviewed for the first time a few days earlier. She had just received a typed letter purportedly from Suzette that had been postmarked from San Jose, California, on March 27. Carolyn explained that this letter, like the e-mails

216. Herrman went into the back room and returned with the tape from March 1. The time shown on the tape, he said, was approximately one hour and eleven minutes fast.

Pierce also spoke to housekeeping staffers, who told him Suzette had discarded a number of bloody sheets and towels during her stay. One of them, Isabel Paulin, who would later marry and take her husband's name, Clark, said it was as though she'd been on her period for more than two weeks, yet it didn't appear that Suzette was in any distress. On the afternoon of March 1, Paulin had also observed a man matching Robinson's description backing his pickup truck into a parking space outside Suzette's room and loading it with belongings from the room where she stayed.

Back at the station that afternoon, Pierce popped the hotel videotape into a VCR and several detectives watched with excitement as the balding, pudgy man they knew as Robinson entered the front lobby and dropped the keys on the front desk. The time on the tape was 4:19 P.M. or—accounting for the fact that it was fast—3:08 P.M. It was consistent with the time, 3:04 P.M., that the Guesthouse Suites had swiped Robinson's credit card to pay for the room. Suzette was nowhere in sight, they noted.

While Pierce was at the Guesthouse Suites, Brad Hill had been calling kennels, animal shelters and storage lockers all over town. He hit pay dirt with the ninth locker on his list: Needmor Storage, located on North Kansas City Road in Olathe. Speaking with manager Linda Harvey, he learned that Robinson had rented a 10' x 15' locker, B-18, on June 5, 1998. Hill was able to obtain the activity log for the gates of the storage units. Robinson had entered the gate on March 1 at 2:24 P.M. and left six minutes later.

Hill got another break when Tina Clark, the animal control officer (ACO) for the Olathe Police Department, remembered colleague Rodney McClain picking up two Pekingese at Santa Barbara Estates. Calling the trailer park's front office, he was transferred to a woman named Nancy, who said her husband

over her shoulder. "Carolyn told me that those dogs meant everything to her daughter—they were her babies," said Brown, who had begun talking to Suzette's mother on a regular basis. "If Harry and Peka were found without Suzette nearby, something was very seriously wrong."

Preparing to meet with the family in Michigan, Brown decided to wait and deliver the bad news in person.

Meanwhile, Owsley was up to his ears in trash. Beginning on March 31, the narcotics detective would stop by the trailer court around 4:00 A.M. on Tuesdays and Fridays. After replacing Robinson's garbage with identical bags, he would return to the Lenexa police station and meticulously sort through the refuse, keeping only what he thought was of evidentiary value.

Owsley got a surprise in his very first pickup when he opened one of the bags and discovered a separate plastic bag full of shredded paper. Working at long tables in two-hour shifts, detectives went through each strand and started piles according to colors, types and lengths of paper. As the piles grew, detectives began matching the individual shreds. By April 4, Layman was able to photocopy eighteen documents they had reassembled. They provided a wealth of information: phone bills, credit cards, checking accounts, e-mail addresses and—most valuable of all—a bill for another storage facility, Stor-Mor For Less, on 58 Highway over the state line in Raymore, Missouri.

Roth assigned Pierce to follow up on the Raymore locker. From manager Loretta Mattingly, he learned that in 1993 Nancy Robinson had rented locker 23. Then Mattingly casually dropped a bombshell: Nancy's husband had rented a second locker, E-2, in the name of Beverly J. Bonner back in January 1994. At the time, Robinson said Bonner was his sister and he was storing her belongings while she lived in Australia. Funny, though, Mattingly couldn't remember ever meeting Bonner. She also noted that Robinson instructed her never to send the bill for this locker to his home. Instead, he

Texas. During the lapse in surveillance, they had missed her visit.

Through credit card bills, detectives also learned that on April 5 Robinson had charged another hotel room in Clinton, Missouri. Initially they had no idea what he had been doing there—until, that is, they applied for and received a court order on April 14 that allowed them to begin monitoring Robinson's cell phone activity. Though they couldn't listen in on the conversations, they could now at least determine whom he was calling and when. It didn't take them long to identify a woman in nearby Springfield—Linda G.—as Robinson's mystery date.

Both incidents sparked heated debates on how the detectives could possibly protect the women coming into town of their own free will to meet Robinson. "It was true that they were grown women and making these rendezvous on their own," Roth said. "But the thought of him hurting or killing someone chilled us to the core." It also made them appreciate the importance of surveillance, which they had restarted on April 10. "We had been lucky," he added. "Two women had been with Robinson in motels. They were alive but not because we knew about it."

While Brown flew to Michigan on April 13 to meet with the Trouten family, his unit at home put the mystery of the missing dogs completely to rest. Robinson's MasterCard bills, which came in the mail through subpoena the same day, revealed not only a transaction for Guesthouse Suites but also one for Ridgeview Animal Hospital. Boyer and Meyer collected paperwork from the animal clinic showing that Robinson had claimed to be Suzette's employer as he checked in the dogs on February 16. He, not Suzette, checked them out on March 1 at 2:13 P.M.

On April 14, 2000, surveillance officers again followed Robinson to the Grant Avenue address in Overland Park. After a forty-five-minute visit, he exited the duplex about 2:00 P.M. A plump, middle-aged woman with shoulder-length reddish

were specifically issued to the account of John Robinson while he was online."

Likewise, the subpoenaed records from Email.com confirmed that Remington was right in suspecting that Robinson was posing as JT or James R. Turner using the "eruditemaster" address. After comparing the logins at Grapevine to those for Email.com, Hill said, "it was determined that the same IP address was in use by the account of John Robinson."

Detectives now had proof that their suspect was using the Internet to pose as ficticious individuals as well as one person who was real: Suzette. "For me," Brown said, "That was, 'Okay, we gotcha, ya bastard.'"

By this point, Roth had decided to run the Robinson investigation like a "Metro Squad" case, a concept that began under Chief Clarence Kelly and the Kansas City, Missouri, police department in the 1960s. The idea was to bring together detectives from several agencies to crack a big case—usually involving a homicide. Brown, who suggested the idea, thought it made sense since Overland Park was already involved and there could well be other jurisdictions before they were done.

Typically, in a Metro Squad case, a sergeant would write a lead on an index card and give it to a detective to investigate. When the detective was done, he or she would turn in the lead card and an accompanying report. Within a couple of days, Brown helped Roth load special computer software onto his laptop and from then on the lead cards were automated. "This may not seem like a big deal," Roth said, "but when the leads reached into the hundreds, it was a lifesaver."

The first days and weeks also led to many differences of opinion among investigators and prosecutors—as most complex cases do. There was a continuous string of closed-door meetings. One of the first issues they had to face was what kind of case they had. Some thought Suzette had been sold into "white slavery" or was being held somewhere against her will. Others were convinced she was already dead. The way they leaned would determine how to pursue the case:

Chapter 5

There was nothing obvious in John Edward Robinson Sr.'s childhood that suggested to detectives he would one day become a serial killer. Born two days after Christmas in 1943, his parents had introduced him to the world in the customary Catholic manner, baptizing him at Mary Queen of Heaven, their parish church in the bleak Chicago suburb of Cicero. Church records show that family friends William Conway and Johanna Harwell stepped in as proxies when godparents Edward and Agnes Robinson couldn't attend the April ceremony.

Henry Robinson Sr. worked as a machinist for Western Electric Company's Hawthorne Works, whose large stacks often belched thick black smoke into the air of the staunchly working-class community. His wife, Alberta, was a homemaker who had her hands full raising five children. Henry junior led the brood, followed by Joann, John, Mary Ellen and Donald. They lived in a three-story modest home on West Thirty-second Street—in a neighborhood of corner bars, tree-lined streets and the famous Sportsman's Park Race Track, which drew crowds of gamblers and drinkers from all over Chicago.

John Robinson would later describe his family in contradictory terms. Talking to prison psychiatrists in 1987, he referred to them as "traditional American," saying he respected them for their accomplishments and had felt great support throughout his lifetime to achieve great things. "He could think of nothing negative to include which would

welcome to the Eagle High Court of Honor of the Chicago Boy Scout Council.

James Krcmarik, of Cicero Explorer Post 2259, led the audience in the Pledge of Allegiance and a prayer of invocation. Then Cornell, Scout executive for the Chicago Boy Scout Council, told the 155 Chicago-area Scouts about to receive their Eagle and Silver awards that they were the city's "elite" future leaders. "The kind of a city that Chicago will be is in your hands," he said. "It can be beautiful or ugly, clean or filthy, honest or corrupt."

John Robinson's parents sat in the audience, proudly watching as their son, along with sixteen other Scouts, filed to the podium to receive their Eagle badges. "We were like the youngest Eagle Scouts ever made," recalled Krcmarik, who received his badge with John that day. "He wasn't a big guy. He was a little guy. He was kind of quiet and nondescript."

Somehow, however, the "quiet and nondescript" boy managed to finagle his way into representing American Scouts in a royal variety show put on for the queen of England. Eleven days after receiving his Eagle badge, as several newspapers reported, John Robinson flew to London to begin rehearsals for a dazzling three-hour production that included Judy Garland and legendary British actress Gracie Fields.

According to an article in the *Cicero Life* newspaper, John Robinson—then a freshman at Quigley Preparatory Seminary—was chosen for a singing scene from the Boy Scouts' own *Gang Show* because of his scholastic ability, scouting experience and poise. "Besides having a bright and friendly smile, John sings in the choir at Holy Name Cathedral and Quigley Seminary," the article stated.

His trip even made the front page of the *London Daily Sketch* and the *Chicago Tribune,* which proclaimed him as one of its own: CHICAGO BOY SCOUT LEADS TROOP TO SING FOR QUEEN. In the article, journalist Arthur Veysey described a cocky John Robinson trading quips with Judy Garland before the show. "We Americans gotta stick together," Robinson said

way the English talked. He also said he enjoyed meeting the queen and seeing London, but it was nice to be home. In a scene of apparent domestic tranquillity, a smiling Robinson was pictured posing with his heavyset mother, Alberta, as she looked through a souvenir album while his blond-haired younger sister, Mary Ellen, adjusted his Scottish tam.

Things, however, were not going so smoothly for John at Quigley, the imposing Gothic-looking institution in downtown Chicago founded in 1905 to educate the city's future priests. As a freshman, John was required to take Latin, English, algebra I, general science, physical education (consisting of tumbling, wrestling, swimming and track), music (studying the "fundamentals of Gregorian chant and intelligent appreciation of modern music") and, of course, religion. "The seminarian learns from the spiritual directors how to love Christ and his Church, and how to order his life as a seminarian," states the 1958 Quigley yearbook, *Le Petit Seminaire*. "Nevertheless, before such action and love must come a solid knowledge of the Faith, a knowledge supplied by the religion course at Quigley. This course includes the study of Catholic dogma, or morals, and of the different forms of religious worship, with special emphasis on the Mass."

John, who had a just above average IQ of 102, was flunking out of the academically demanding school. According to school records, his attendance was good—except for the two weeks he was in London—but he had failed both semesters of Latin and algebra I and received a grade of Poor in English and religion, Satisfactory in general science and Good only in physical education and music. Most telling, however, was his grade for deportment, which was Excellent in the first quarter but had slipped twenty-two points by the end of the year to Poor. He finished the year at the bottom of his class, ranking 379 out of 390 students.

"You did not have to be a 'genius' to succeed at the school," said one former classmate, who did not wish to be identified. "But you first did have to pass an entrance exam to win

son met Barbara Sandre, then a fifteen-year-old Canadian girl who had become involved in a Toronto production of the Boy Scouts' *Gang Show*. On the last night of the show, May 12, there was a cast party and Robinson, who had come from Chicago with several other Scouts to see the production, had been invited. Though they saw each other just that one night, the two began a correspondence and a romance that would span not only continents but also decades.

Back in Chicago, however, John Robinson apparently fell in love with a pretty blond wisp of a girl named Nancy Jo Lynch. After a whirlwind three-month courtship, they married in March 1964 and, within the year, moved to Kansas City and began raising a family. Their first child, John junior, was born in January 1965, followed by daughter Kimberly in April 1967 and twins Chris and Christine in May 1971. By then, the young father of four had already experienced several run-ins with the law.

his short stint at Children's Mercy. But it was hardly the last time that Bermel would hear about her confident, cheerful coworker.

In April 1966, Robinson managed to talk his way into an even better job, actually running the lab at Fountain Plaza X-Ray Laboratory, owned by Dr. Wallace Graham, who had an upstairs medical office. Graham, who died in 1996, had impeccable credentials, as an Eagle Scout, local Golden Gloves boxing champ, World War II hero and the personal friend and physician to former president Harry Truman.

He could also be accommodating to a fault. In 1946, Truman wrote a note to Dr. Graham's father in which he praised "that son of yours" but also warned: "The young doctor will work himself to death if he lets all the chiselers take advantage of him."

Robinson, chief among chiselers, apparently saw his opportunity. Dr. Graham's son, then a fifteen-year-old lab technician working summers for his father, remembers his new boss as a "can-do guy."

"He had all these papers saying he was board certified by the American Board of Radiology and he had all these references," recalled Dr. Bruce Graham, now a successful colon and rectal surgeon. "He looked good on paper and he really put on a good show. He was very confident, very articulate and pleasant. He was also an Eagle Scout, which impressed my father very much."

The younger Dr. Graham added that his father was the kind of man who, once he felt comfortable, would let someone take the ball and run with it. "That was my dad's way of doing business," he said. "He was not a micromanager, and he had an extremely busy practice."

By Christmas, 1966, though, Dr. Wallace Graham was losing so much money that he couldn't afford to award holiday bonuses. While fellow employees worried about the grim finances, court records later stated, Robinson bragged of buying lakefront property, horses, a Saint Bernard and a new car for his

thought it was around two hundred thousand or more, but we could only prove thirty-three thousand dollars," he said. In the end, Robinson got off with a slap on the wrists, receiving just three years' probation. And though he was ordered to pay full restitution, Dr. Graham said, "We never got a cent."

Shortly after Robinson's firing, Bermel—of all people—answered a classified ad seeking his replacement at Fountain Plaza X-Ray Laboratory. She took the job and was impressed by all of the certificates and diplomas still hanging on the walls of her new office. "I was in awe," she said. "I thought, 'Wow, this guy was really educated. I don't know if I'm going to be able to [fill his shoes.]'"

Cleaning out the X-ray darkroom, however, Bermel came across a box and was stunned as she looked inside to see hundreds of blank certificates wrapped in cellophane. After showing them to Dr. Graham, she said, "He was in shock. He asked, 'Where did you get these from?'" When she told him, Dr. Graham shook his head and said, "I always thought he was awfully young to have all of those degrees."

Not long afterward, Bermel received an eye-opening long-distance call. "They asked for [Robinson]," she said. "I asked who was calling and it was some doctors in Chicago who said he had stolen from them, too, and he had been paying restitution, but they hadn't received any money for some time." Later on, she heard a similar story from another doctor, a podiatrist in Kansas City. "This young man really turned out to be a terrible, terrible crook!" she exclaimed.

By the fall of 1969, Robinson had obtained a new job as systems analyst at the Kansas City office of Mobil Oil Corporation (Ironically, a woman named Beverly Lake—later known as Beverly Bonner—was also working there.) Probation Officer Douglas Pimm remarked in a progress report that Robinson was earning $760 a month at his new job and "they are not aware of his probation status."

This did not seem to worry Pimm, who noted that Robinson "does not appear to be an individual who is basically

rested and, this time, thrown in jail for two weeks when he failed to notify the parole board of the change in his residence and employment. Robinson's probation officer demanded that he make a complete turnaround in his daily behavior or the parole board would have to revoke his probation and consider him a menace to society—due to his constant lying, cheating and stealing. "Prior to 9-8-71 Robinson had never served any jail time," wrote Probation Officer Gordon Morris. "Thus it was felt that a period of time in Jail, combined with extensive counseling, would be a sufficient force to not only catch his attention but to provide a strong motivation for a complete reversal in his behavior."

Robinson apparently fooled the probation officer—much like he would many others down the road. "[He] has been making some definite progress in the reorientation to his thinking," Morris continued, "and thus we feel that Robinson is now ready to function once again in society."

Even so, however, he recommended that Robinson remain under strict supervision—securing a type of employment that could be checked by a probation officer for any "abnormal deviations," having his wife handle all of the family financial transactions and bookkeeping and attending regular group therapy sessions. A judge agreed to extend his probation by two years, though it's not clear if Robinson adhered to any of his probation officer's recommendations.

By this time, Robinson had decided to go into business for himself, with a company called the Professional Services Association, Inc., (PSA), which was supposed to provide financial consulting to doctors in the Kansas City area. Two groups of doctors at the University of Kansas Medical Center hired Robinson to manage their financial affairs but quickly dismissed him because of accounting irregularities.

Undaunted, Robinson continued to send letters to potential investors, portraying PSA as a thriving firm. He even had his young secretary, Charlotte Bowersock, draft a couple of fake letters in what would result in one of his most unsuccessful scams.

tion with a proven program in the service industry looking for individual who will assist in developing the program nation-wide," the ad read. "If you are a go getter, willing to invest in your own future and want to make your own opportunities for financial security. Call Monday."

Whenever Robinson received a reply, he would send out a PSA prospectus that contained the two forged letters. Anyone with inside information that the publicly owned pharmaceutical giant was planning a takeover of PSA could make a killing. Though the letters were a hoax, Robinson could still make money by convincing unsuspecting investors to buy shares of his worthless company stock.

One of those investors was the late Prairie Village businessman Mac F. Cahal. When Cahal called Robinson, he received not only the prospectus but also a balance sheet that vastly inflated the value of PSA's training and reference manuals, which were the company's only assets. Unluckily for the con man, however, Cahal also happened to be good friends with Ewing Kauffman and called him after sending off a $2,500 down payment for ten thousand shares of PSA at $1 apiece. Kauffman "hit the ceiling," Cahal later told *The Kansas City Star*. He immediately stopped payment on his check and called the U.S. Securities and Exchange Commission, which opened an investigation into Robinson's stock solicitation scam.

In December 1975, a federal grand jury indicted Robinson on four counts of securities and mail fraud. Five months later, he pleaded no contest to reduced charges and Judge John W. Oliver fined him $2,500, placing him on another three years' probation. "He was engaging in schemes that, in my view, pretty much ensured he would get caught," said Bruce Houdek, Robinson's lawyer on that particular case. "He was a small-time, penny-ante con guy who spent more time getting out of trouble than getting into it—and he got into trouble pretty easily."

retired and with his wife dying of cancer, agreed to invest in Hydro-Gro. At the time, Nancy was in her early twenties and an aspiring artist and Robinson allowed her to illustrate his how-to gardening booklet. "He was very nice to me, very encouraging," she later told *The Kansas City Star*. Ultimately her father and other family members invested more than $5,000. An aunt reportedly sunk $20,000. They would never recoup a dime.

In his new community, Robinson held himself out as a leader, taking an active role in Scouting, The Presbyterian Church of Stanley and other civic engagements. In December 1977, he even received a commendation from the mayor for his work with the handicapped and was named Man of the Year at a luncheon sponsored by a local "sheltered workshop association" and attended by the former state Senator Mary Gant. GROUP FOR DISABLED HONORS AREA MAN was the headline in the December 8 edition of *The Kansas City Times*. Two weeks later, however, *The Kansas City Star*—then the afternoon paper—revealed that the event was just another of Robinson's schemes. With the headline, MAN-OF-THE-YEAR PLOY BACKFIRES ON HONOREE," the story provided details of how Robinson had engineered the entire affair—down to his Man of the Year plaque—through an elaborate sequence of fake letters of recommendation sent to city hall.

The following year, in 1978, Margaret Adams saw Robinson at a downtown trade show, where he was demonstrating his hydroponic kits and giving away beautiful-looking tomatoes. Moving with her family to Pleasant Valley, the avid gardener soon discovered that Robinson was her new neighbor and asked him to demonstrate his hydroponics systems. "He couldn't have been nicer," Margaret said, until she told him the kit was out of her price range. With a withering glance, he snapped that she was "small potatoes" and had wasted his time. "He was rather sharp and could put you down with just a look or a comment," she said. "I found out later that that was his way of controlling people."

As neighbors soon discovered, Robinson was a man who

The mischievous twins would steal the go-cart belonging to their neighbor Dorothy Davis and drive it up and down the street for hours, causing Hilary and her parents to break into laughter as they watched their antics. Christy also loved to help Margaret Adams pick the strawberries in her garden. "She was a tiny little thing and she would tiptoe around the strawberry bed," she recalled. "She was a sweet little girl, very small, and I'd say, 'It's only fair that you get half.'"

John junior was very nice, Hilary said, and quite different from his father in that he didn't seem to rub anyone the wrong way. "He was into the theater, always in some play or musical, and very left-brained, more artistic," she remembered, adding that he always wore his Scouting uniform to school, which she thought was quite geeky. Kim, on the other hand, was more reserved. "When I think of Kim, I think of a straight A student," Hilary said. "She was extremely smart, very studious and quiet."

In 1980, Robinson, who had put Hydro-Gro on the back burner, took a job as the personnel manager at a Liberty, Missouri, subsidiary of Borden, Inc., known as Guy's Foods. James Caldwell, the operations manager until the company went belly up in 2001, remembered the period as chaotic. Borden had recently bought the snack food company and, somehow, no one bothered to run a background check. "He was the personnel manager and they're typically outgoing, friendly and very helpful people and that's the way he was," said Caldwell. "He also embezzled a lot of money."

At the time, Borden had just decided to sell its fleet of Ford Econoline vans and was offering them to its salesmen and other employees at very good prices. Caldwell, whose uncle had founded the snack food company, got the first clue that something was wrong when he started getting calls from employees who wanted to know if he had received their checks for the vans they had purchased from Robinson. He tracked their checks—and several others—to a dummy bank account disguised to look like a legitimate corporate account. "John Robinson had set it up in his name and he was the only one

He smiled and waved at me—as if to say, 'I got out of it.' It sent chills down my spine."

Back in Pleasant Valley Farms, Nancy Robinson had confided in Scott Davis's mother, Dorothy, that she knew about Becky and had started divorce proceedings. (She later reconsidered after the couple received marital counseling.) "My mom and [Nancy] became good friends and through that I heard a lot," said Scott Davis, now a computer consultant. "I knew he was having an affair [with Becky] because I was asked by Nancy to follow his car to see where he went. But I couldn't keep up with him and I lost him."

Neighbors later learned that Robinson had also tried to grope a woman who lived in the subdivision. When the woman immediately reported the incident to her husband, her spouse became furious and headed to confront Robinson. Robinson saw him coming, though, and jumped in his car and took off. The woman's husband—a giant of a man—followed him for miles. "I think he would have torn John's head off," said one of the neighbors. "But John was good at getting away."

On May 8, 1982, Robinson arrived at the Clay County Court to start his sixty-day sentence. Davis said the Robinson family tried their best to keep a lid on the embarrassing situation. "I don't think everybody knew, but a lot of people did," Davis recalled. "I was told, 'Hush, hush.'" Robinson and his wife actually told their kids he was going away on a "business trip"—though by the look on their faces as they boarded the school bus, Hilary Adams figured they knew the truth. "It was kind of scandalous in a neighborhood where most of the fathers were executives working for Bendix [Corporation] or Marion Labs," she said.

Upon his release in July, the convict was as cocky as ever. "He hadn't learned any lessons," Scott Davis said. "There was no shame or remorse. In fact, he came back bragging about the contacts he'd made there." Davis said Robinson had also bragged to him about inventing the phantom employees at Guy's Foods and even demonstrated his expertise at forgery, showing him how to use a Xerox copy machine, whiteout and

The meeting with the bank president made Scott Davis even more suspicious that something shady was going on. They handed the president a business proposition. He asked a few questions and then told them to leave while the attorney stayed behind to finalize the loan. "It was so perfunctory, it wasn't even funny," Davis remembered. "There was no discussion of the details, no due diligence, none of the things you would expect in a normal business transaction." Davis waited a week, then two. Finally calling the bank, he learned that it had closed down and the Feds were investigating.

By 1983, Davis and his father were forced to file chapter 7, which only served to infuriate Robinson, who hadn't received any real money for his services. According to Davis, Robinson's response was to forge some documents that said Bob Davis had agreed to pay him $125,000 no matter what happened to the company. Scott Davis, who said he was all too familiar with Robinson's cut-and-paste talents, demanded that he produce the original. "He never did," Davis said.

Then Robinson wanted to handle the liquidation and went so far as to organize the creditors, putting himself at the top of the list. "He wanted to get paid first," Davis said. "He went to my bankruptcy attorney and said, 'Wouldn't it be nice if I went to the head of the line?' "

When that didn't work, Robinson left an angry letter to Dorothy Davis on her doorstep, stating that he was organizing the creditors to fight and warning her that she would lose her home if he didn't get his money. "John could talk to you for an hour and know what buttons to push," Scott Davis said. "And that was a button with my mother."

Ultimately, though, the Davis family refused to pay him a cent. And Robinson, looking for other fish to fry, moved on. Expanding upon Equi-Plus, he formed a new company, Equi-II, which engaged in a variety of so-called management consultant and philanthropic ventures. This time, however, Robinson would not only use his companies to defraud and steal. He would use them for something more sinister.

end without telling the family. Her father, Bill, who had been away on a business trip when Paula left, drove to the Equi-II office in the Windmill Square Shopping Center in Overland Park to question Robinson about his daughter's whereabouts. Robinson, he said, was in his office with a middle-aged receptionist and told him he hadn't heard from her since he sent her for training. He didn't know where she was.

Within a few days, the Godfreys received a handwritten letter, purportedly from their daughter, who apologized for not calling and explained she had some things she needed to work out for herself. She told them she was fine and that she would call as soon as she could get her "head on straight."

"Maybe then we can all sit down and talk and be a family again," she wrote, telling her parents to say hello to her sister and brother.

Though the handwriting looked authentic, the Godfreys had a gut feeling after receiving the note that something was very wrong. "We thought it was very out-of-character for her," Bill Godfrey later told *The Kansas City Star*. "We weren't mad at her, and she wasn't mad at us. She was a mature young lady looking to get involved in business."

Bill Godfrey told police he returned to the Equi-II office. With the same middle-aged receptionist as a witness, Godfrey said, he pointed a .32-caliber handgun at Robinson and angrily threatened to kill him if he did not receive a telephone call from his daughter Paula within three days. Robinson reportedly became very nervous and said he would get word to Paula to call home—which sounded strange coming from a man who previously professed not to know where she was.

No phone call ever came. However, the Godfreys would receive two more letters from Paula that didn't seem to make much sense. In the letters, both handwritten in September, she referred to the great time she was having with a girlfriend named "Jackie"; her parents didn't have a clue who Jackie was. Godfrey's wife talked her husband out of going back to see Robinson, convincing him to sell the gun and leave the

in mid-December and Carl returned to service in the navy, just outside of Chicago, a few days after Christmas.

Lisa and Tiffany checked into Hope House, a shelter for battered women, but kept in touch with Carl's family and other relatives. Kathy Klinginsmith, his sister, agreed to watch her four-month-old niece after Lisa dropped by on January 8, 1985. Before she went out for the evening, Lisa told Kathy about a Johnson County businessman, "John Osborne," who was purportedly involved with helping young mothers. Osborne, Lisa said, wanted to help her get her GED and find a job. He was also putting her up in the Rodeway Inn in Overland Park, which raised Kathy's eyebrows. "I told her she ought to be cautious because, for one, she didn't know him all that well," she later testified. "She didn't know what his intentions were."

After spending the evening at a neighborhood bar and her in-laws' house, Lisa returned to Kathy's house the next day and called the front desk of the Rodeway Inn. Osborne was looking for her. She left a message for him to call her at the Klinginsmiths'. When the phone rang a few minutes later, Kathy gave Osborne directions to her house. While they waited, Lisa mentioned that Osborne had bought train tickets to go to Chicago that week about a job. A stocky man with brown hair, glasses and a deep voice arrived just twenty-five minutes later—driving across the city through a bad snowstorm to fetch Lisa and her baby. Osborne didn't waste any time on pleasantries, insisting they leave immediately. "He didn't say a word to me," Kathy Klinginsmith later said. "Nothing. He was just evil."

Lisa carried Tiffany to Osborne's car, which was parked down the street and out of view, leaving her own yellow Toyota Corolla and most of her belongings behind. Kathy's five-year-old son seemed petrified of Osborne, which only served to frighten her more. "I wanted to run after her and get her, but I was too scared," Kathy Klinginsmith said. "I was afraid of him. I knew deep down that was the last time I would see Lisa."

Betty Stasi, Lisa's mother-in-law, received a call later that night. "I took it for granted she was at her motel," she later tes-

Chapter 9

Stephen Haymes had picked up Robinson's trail just before Lisa and Tiffany went missing. It all started with a disturbing call the soft-spoken mustachioed probation supervisor received on December 18, 1984, from Ann Smith at Birthright. Smith told Haymes that Robinson had approached her organization, saying he was on the board of directors of an Olathe bank and affiliated with The Presbyterian Church of Stanley, Kansas, which was developing a program to help young women who had just delivered babies. The church, he had explained, wished to place young mothers in a duplex in Olathe and pay their expenses while they got back on their feet. Robinson wanted to know if anyone at Birthright might fit the profile.

Smith told Haymes she became suspicious and decided to check out Robinson's story when he became insistent upon finding a young mother by December 24. Calling the church, she learned that Robinson was a member of the congregation but he was not representing them in any way and they had no program to help young women. Likewise, the bank said Robinson did not sit on its board of directors. In fact, as Smith relayed to Haymes, the bank had never heard of him. Upon learning that he was on probation out of Clay County, Missouri—on the old Guy's Foods conviction—Smith had called the Missouri Board of Probation and Parole and been connected to Haymes, the district supervisor.

Haymes also had never heard of Robinson, for his office in Liberty, Missouri, had transferred Robinson's supervision by means of an interstate compact agreement to a probation

fortunate than himself. "I didn't buy the story," Haymes said. "Probably because I'm cynical." He paused to laugh. "But a certain amount of cynicism is healthy in this profession. I didn't believe that a person who had a history of embezzling money was going to be giving to charities. He was also too good of a talker. Little things didn't match up. He would twist the truth—not enough to make it blatantly obvious he was lying but just enough that you'd have to go out and reinvestigate that what he was telling you wasn't true."

Haymes subsequently spoke with Gaddis and learned that while the two black women were doing well, a young white woman and her baby had gone missing after staying in an Overland Park hotel. Detectives, he said she told him, were investigating. "Gaddis cautioned this officer that there was some question about the program as the white girl that they had helped to arrange placement with had disappeared approximately three weeks earlier," wrote Haymes, whose careful notes about Robinson would later be filed in Clay County Circuit Court.

When Haymes called the Overland Park police, Detective Larry Dixon told him that they had been unable so far to find any evidence of wrongdoing in the Stasi investigation. The detective also mentioned that a second young woman who had worked for Robinson—Paula Godfrey—had been reported missing a few months earlier, but they had received a letter from her stating that she did not want to see her family. Haymes and Dixon agreed to keep in touch on any new developments in the Robinson case.

When Haymes sat down for another talk with Karen Gaddis and Sharon Jackson Turner on January 30, he learned even more disturbing details. In approaching the social workers before Christmas, John Robinson had stressed the importance of a 50-50 racial mix as this had been stipulated by potential contributors such as Xerox and IBM. Since they had already found two black women for the Troost Avenue apartment, Robinson strongly urged them to find a white

along with Overland Park detective Cindy Scott and the now relentless Haymes were looking into Robinson's activities. While the Stasi leads seemed to be drying up, Haymes recalled that the parolee was creating big trouble for himself on an astonishing number of other fronts.

Larry McClain, then a Johnson County assistant prosecutor and now a disctrict court judge, told Haymes his office was building a case that Robinson's Equi-II had cooked up several phony receipts to defraud a company called Back Care Systems out of about $5,000. McClain also said he had received a complaint from a woman in Kansas City named Mildred Amadi. She said her former landlord, Irv Blattner, had introduced her to Robinson, who claimed he was an attorney and could help her obtain a divorce. Giving him the title to her car as payment, she waited and waited for the divorce papers. "He said . . . I didn't need a copy of the divorce papers," she stated, fuming, when she still hadn't gotten them months later. "He keeps telling me I'm divorced—go out, get married."

Amadi's story convinced Haymes that there was no con too small for Robinson. "He loves the con game," he said. "He loves the challenge of it. And it doesn't always matter what he wins. Here he took a 1970s American Motors Pacer, which was probably the worst car in history, as payment for his services as an 'attorney,' and that car didn't even run."

Meanwhile, the Secret Service was investigating both Robinson and Blattner, who, as it turned out, was his pal and fellow ex-convict, for forging the signature and cashing a paltry $741 government check. Blattner, however, quickly agreed to help authorities nail Robinson in exchange for lenient treatment.

Haymes felt he had enough evidence at this point to prove Robinson was in clear violation of his parole. Ordered to appear for another visit, on March 21, Haymes informed him that he was under arrest and would be transported to the Clay County Jail. "I had just put handcuffs on him," he remembered, "and he'd gotten very, very nervous and panicky about having gotten arrested. He didn't like the thought of going

described by the women as "twenty-seven years old, blond and fat," also worked for Robinson.

Based on these and other interviews, investigators came to believe that Robinson was attempting to organize a ring of prostitutes and that Equi-II was more of an escort service than a consulting company. Boothroyd and Blattner, they realized, were both involved in recruiting women for Robinson, who would typically take them to a hotel, photograph them in various stages of undress and often require sex before hiring them. Prostitution, however, was just the tip of the iceberg.

Williams contacted Boothroyd because she had lost the piece of paper with Robinson's phone number. Though Boothroyd gave it to her, he also told her not to trust Robinson because "he could get [her] hurt." Calling him anyway, they met at the McDonald's next to the Laundromat where she worked. In the course of their conversation, she said, he offered to put her up in an apartment and take care of her financially if she would be his mistress. He also allegedly agreed to supply her with money and marijuana.

At the end of April 1985, Williams said, Robinson came to the Laundromat and handed her the keys to the Troost Avenue apartment, which by this time had been vacated by the two black women, and instructed her to leave work and never go back. "He told me our relationship must be kept quiet and wanted to always be sure that we were not seen together in public," she said.

There was at least one reason for Robinson's secrecy. After a long investigation, Johnson County had charged him in late March with felony theft by deception in the Back Care Systems case. After posting a $10,000 bond, he had been released on his own recognizance. Upon learning this, Haymes had written a second violation report, again recommending that Robinson's Missouri probation be revoked. Haymes, who kept hearing from Gaddis and other social workers about Robinson's continued attempts to find women with babies, had also asked Robinson on several occasions if he had gotten rid of the Troost Avenue apartment. He lied and said that he had.

Meanwhile, Robinson dropped by the apartment and asked Williams for a favor. Bringing out S&M equipment, he put roach clips on her nipples and asked if they hurt. He then told her that one of his customers in the escort business was into S&M and needed a girl for about a week. He brought out a whip made of cat-o'-nine tails and hit her with it on the leg so she could see how it felt. He also had her get dressed and they left the house. "When we were outside, I again pulled down the blindfold," she said. "I did not see streetlights and the house we had just left was off by itself; it was all dark around the area."

Back in her apartment, she counted the money the driver had put in her purse; there was $1,200. She went out to buy some booze and subsequently passed out. Meeting with Robinson the next day, she told him what happened and that she had spent some of the money. He let her keep another $50, she said, and told her not to worry about the incident. "He then consoled me for a while and left," she stated. "Before leaving, he said he would be out of town for a while."

Toward the end of May 1985, Robinson returned to the apartment and told Theresa he wanted to play a joke on his friend Irv Blattner. He told her to buy a diary and he would tell her what to write. "He gave me a manuscript that he had written with dates and entries for me to write in my own handwriting," said Williams, who started to work on her assignment.

When Robinson didn't return for ten days, though, Williams called an old boyfriend to bring her some food. While he was there, she said, Robinson appeared. The boyfriend hid in the second bedroom, but Robinson somehow figured out he was there and angrily told her he didn't want her seeing him until after 4:00 P.M. on weekdays.

Robinson let himself into Williams's apartment early the next morning, a Saturday, while she was sleeping. Entering her room, he grabbed her and put her over his knee to spank her, she said. "He said I had been a real bad girl and needed to learn a lesson." Apparently, he was still angry about her boyfriend's visit. While she yelled and screamed, he pulled her hair and threw her down on the floor. He took his gun, which Williams had seen him carry in a shoulder holster, and held it to her head. "I'll blow your brains out if you don't stop screaming," he threatened, then shoved

watching the apartment, paid a fortuitous visit. At first she lied and told them she worked for Robinson at Equi-II. However, after the FBI agents told her they believed her "boss" was involved in the disappearance of two women, she broke into tears and admitted everything. She told them about their upcoming trip to the Bahamas and how she was at that very moment fabricating a diary that accused Blattner of committing various crimes and threatening her life. The last entry in the diary was June 15.

The agents quickly suspected that Robinson somehow knew his partner (who would die of cancer in 1991) was about to testify against him and planned to use the fake diary to try and discredit him. Williams's life was most certainly in danger. To everyone's surprise, Robinson at that very moment unlocked the front door and entered the apartment. Holding up his draft of the diary, Lavin and Dancer identified themselves and asked Robinson if it was his handwriting. He admitted that it was, then beat a hasty retreat. The agents didn't attempt to stop him but insisted on moving Williams to a secret location. "I get a call from Lavin and Dancer, saying 'Get down here now,'" Haymes recalled. "They were at that moment realizing she was possibly within days of something happening to her."

By that point, Haymes just wanted to get Robinson off the streets to keep him from harming more women. Hearing Williams's story, too, helped him to clarify what had probably happened to Lisa and Tiffany. "There was no doubt in my mind that Lisa was dead," Haymes said. "My belief was that he had sold the baby to someone looking to adopt and had sold her into some sort of white slavery or S&M situation that already had or soon would result in her death. At the time, though, I still didn't believe—and I don't think anyone else did, either—that he would kill with his own hands. We believed he would have someone else do his dirty work."

Haymes drafted a third violation report against Robinson, asking the court to put him in jail for carrying a handgun, sup-

Shortly before Robinson went off to prison, however, a third young woman disappeared after telling her family she had found work with Equi-II. According to police records, Robert Bales had picked up his twenty-six-year-old stepsister, Catherine Clampitt, at the Kansas City bus station on a January night in 1987. She reportedly needed a fresh start after a life of drugs and drinking in Wichita Falls, Texas, and Bales and his wife had agreed to put her up in their Overland Park home.

Bales described his stepsister as a petite, intelligent woman with a wild streak. Born in Korea, she had grown up in Texas after being adopted by his mother, Jackie Clampitt. When she moved to Kansas, she left behind a son, Ryan, then three years old, in her parents' custody. Clampitt wasn't in town more than a month when she spotted an ad in *The Kansas City Star* for an executive secretary.

"Extremely busy CEO needs executive secretary /assistant," it read. "International travel required, long hours. Must be attractive, personable and able to devote complete energies to this position." Applicants were instructed to send their resumes to the Overland Park address of Robinson's Equi-II.

Upon landing the job, Clampitt told her stepbrother that her employer was "John Dawson." Once she started working, Bales said, she often traveled and would sometimes stay at local hotels between trips for several nights at a time. She was last at Bales's home between March 16 and April 2, when she left to stay at the Olathe Holiday Inn. She spoke to her stepbrother on April 4 and told him she was at the hotel to do research and would soon be meeting Dawson. They were supposed to drive a van to Chicago, where they would meet another secretary, and fly from there to New York.

Bales later said the job did seem a little far-fetched to him and his wife, but his stepsister was twenty-six and old enough to make her own decisions. "She's a grown lady; you don't lock her in a room and say you can't come out," he reportedly said.

fice. When he did, he was sent to the Overland Park Police Department to file a missing persons report. The police looked into the matter but ultimately couldn't find enough evidence to connect Robinson to Clampitt's disappearance. Bales became consumed with finding her on his own. After eight months, though, he, too, gave up. All the trails were dead ends.

Robinson made a good impression on prison officials during his four-year stay at the Hutchinson Correctional Facility in Kansas. The physical plant supervisor, J.E. Jestes, was reportedly very happy with Robinson's reorganization of the computer maintenance office and the new software program he developed, which Jestes estimated would save Kansas thousands of dollars each year. "Mr. Robinson performed his tasks well, accepted responsibility without question, and is an asset to this office," he wrote in a January 1989 report. "Because of his efforts, even when he leaves, this office should function well."

Inmate #45690 also left a relatively favorable impression with the supervising psychiatrist Dr. George Penn, who headed a team that clinically evaluated the 45-year-old Robinson while he was in Hutchinson. "Mr. Robinson has apparently used his time quite well and been a service to the state in the two years and four months that he has been incarcerated," Dr. Penn wrote. "Mr. Robinson has a very supportive family and says that he has supportive friends. He indicates that at such time as he is eligible for parole, he has been asked to teach X-ray nuclear medicine and medical laboratory procedures at K.U. Medical Center. He says he has been in contact with Dr. Walker and Dr. Peugh at the K.U. Medical Center." Dr. Penn, however, wisely qualified his comments: "This is not verified by this examiner."

Dr. Penn also stated that the inmate had told him about

behavior because he'd gotten off lightly each time. "He has no explanation for his repeated illegal behaviors except to say that he made many poor judgments and at one time was interested in making a lot of money and didn't really care how he went about doing it."

Based on their findings from the available data, Dr. Penn said that it was the opinion of the clinical team that Robinson had "shown some concrete signs of rehabilitation" and that it was "unlikely that further incarceration will be of any benefit to Mr. Robinson or society." However, Dr. Penn recommended that the inmate be restrained from entering into any future business arrangements. While Robinson didn't want to continue the illegal behavior that had been part of his life for such a long time, Dr. Penn said there was no guarantee he wouldn't were he given the opportunity. "He could once again begin by shading the truth and then moving into outright lies and be caught once again in a self-sabotaging, self-defeating situation," he said. "He is a man who is extremely convincing and those working with him need to be very careful less they be seduced by him, wittingly or otherwise."

In 1991, Kansas followed the recommendation of Dr. Penn's team and paroled Robinson, who was turned over to Missouri authorities to determine if he should be freed or face more prison time for violating his Guy's Foods fraud probation a decade earlier. Robinson, of course, claimed that his health had become so frail during his stay at Hutchinson that he should be released to go home to his family. His wife was now managing and living in a mobile home park called Southfork in Belton, Missouri, a south Kansas City suburb. Following her husband's incarceration, she had been forced to move out of her upscale country home in Stanley, Kansas, and single-handedly shoulder the responsibility of supporting herself and her family.

One of Missouri's physicians, Dr. Fred King, agreed with Robinson, saying that the inmate was "an extremely high

misleading information from my file, consider the information available from the Kansas Department of Corrections and all medical recommendations." Without such an order, he concluded, "I will remain in prison. If lucky, I will live long enough to get out but there will be little left. My illnesses are degenerative and, without proper rehabilitation, testing and long term treatment, will continue to get worse. Bruce [Houdek, Robinson's attorney], my family and I all realize that the decision made by the Clay County Court and the Missouri Parole Board amount to a sentence of death. Our only question: it [*sic*] this what is considered proportionate punishment for my crime in Missouri?"

Because of his alleged health problems, Robinson was finally released on house arrest in October 1992 and formally paroled in March 1993. By this point, Haymes was not as concerned about him as he had been back in 1986 and 1987. "No direct threat was ever made," said the probation supervisor, who had exercised caution after the defendant was convicted in Kansas. "But the probation officer that did the pre-sentence [report] in that case called me and said John blamed me for everything and he thought he might attempt to hurt me. So I got cautious. I was aware of who was in the car behind me. I had shown my wife photographs of him and his dark blue Dodge Diplomat. I had two young kids and I made sure they played in the back yard."

By the time he was released from Missouri, however, Robinson appeared to be lying low, supposedly disabled with multiple medical problems. "After he got out, he was supervised by our office in Belton where he lived," Haymes said. "I would check on him periodically but stayed out of it as I did not want to appear to have a personal agenda." After more than two decades of constant run-ins, Robinson would not get into any more trouble with the law until Suzette Trouten went missing seven years later.

When Overland Park detectives Greg Wilson and Scott Weiler began digging into Robinson's history in the spring

Chapter 11

By mid-April 2000, Lenexa detectives had been working six and seven days a week trying to keep track of Robinson. Even with Wilson and Weiler on loan from Overland Park, the suburban police department was stretched to the limit and in dire need of additional forces and equipment. Sergeant John Browning's Directed Patrol Unit came up with the idea of renting dilapidated cars in order to blend better into the scenery during trailer park surveillance. Captain Keith O'Neal's Overland Park Special Investigations Section answered the call for help with surveillance. Beginning on April 17, they would take over most of the evening shifts.

The first night on the job, O'Neal's team followed Robinson and his wife to Toys "R" Us, JCPenney and back home. Given the experience of Lenexa's Directed Patrol Unit, they expected to watch them go to bed and call it a night themselves. But at 10:04 P.M., the white Dodge Ram peeled out of Santa Barbara Estates. "He was just flying down Highway 169," says O'Neal, who estimated his speed between 85 and 90 mph. "We could tell somebody else was in the vehicle with him, but we didn't know who it was. I was thinking, 'Oh my God, what is going on?' "

Waking Roth from a sound sleep, they decided that O'Neal and his team—including Detectives Mike Jacobson, Bill Batt, Jose Carrillo and John Clarke—would follow the Dodge Ram until they could figure out who was with him. Jacobson kept calling the Overland Park dispatch center in an attempt to get a phone number for the sheriff of the particular county they

5:00 P.M. "The man was done for the day," Lowther says. "He was home with Nancy."

By Friday, April 21, 2000, Roth was frustrated. His team had made so many important discoveries in the first few weeks, but now he felt as though the investigation was losing momentum. Things weren't going well on the home front, either—it probably didn't help that he was always working—and he was about to leave town to attend a four-day training session with the Kansas Narcotics Officers Association. After joining the other detectives for "Fat Friday," a weekly tradition of doughnuts, reading newspapers and shooting the breeze, Roth took a very long drive. "The case was going very, very slow," he remembered. "Things at home were about as bad as they could get, and I was going to be away the following week. Could it get any worse?"

Back at the station, Dave Brown was waiting for Roth with a new development from Michigan. The detective had recently returned from his trip, where he had met with Suzette's mother, sisters and grandmother and broken the news about the dogs, which had been very difficult for the family. While he shared with the Troutens that Robinson had been convicted of a number of financial crimes, Brown withheld the fact that he had also been linked to three missing women and a baby. Amidst tears, the family reiterated their belief that Suzette was dead or being held somewhere against her will. Before he left, Brown had shown Carolyn Trouten how to record a phone call. They tried, without success, to reach Robinson.

After Brown's return to Kansas, however, Carolyn paged Robinson again and got lucky. When he phoned back a short while later, it was clear he didn't realize to whom he was speaking. She had caught him completely off guard. Knowing Robinson was aware of Suzette's promise to send her a doll from each exotic spot they visited, Carolyn told him a lie and said she had received one, when in fact she hadn't. She wanted to see how he would react. Roth was furious when he heard about the call, fearful that she had aroused

Chapter 12

Vickie Neufeld was feeling lonely and down on her luck in the spring of 2000. The last five years had taken their toll on the blond Tennessee therapist, starting in 1995 when her husband of nineteen years asked her to move out. Busy raising two children and working towards her doctorate in clinical psychology, Vickie had ignored rumors that he was seeing another woman.

She moved by herself into a nearby apartment, saddened at having to leave behind her teenage son and daughter. She knew there was a good chance she would soon have to move out of town to find work, however, and she didn't want to uproot them. As Vickie struggled with her dissertation, her ex-husband remarried the other woman. "The grief was unbearable at times," she said.

Her $30,000 divorce settlement was almost gone by the time Vickie earned her doctorate in August 1998, yet she still needed to complete a one-year residency in order to become licensed. Vickie knew she couldn't afford to be choosy. That meant moving in late 1999 to Galveston, Texas, where she had been offered work counseling the elderly in nearby Houston. Vickie didn't care much for Texas and disliked the residency even more; the feeling apparently was mutual. She wasn't kept on at the end of a ninety-day probationary period.

Vickie filed for unemployment benefits, sent out dozens of resumes and even went on a handful of promising interviews. Nothing panned out. Then, in late March 2000, she was denied unemployment, which she had been counting on while

employed' because I felt like that situation would be temporary," she said. But when no job materialized, she started to tell those who responded that she was out of work and might have to move in the next few months. "It's not a good time to get involved in a relationship with anyone right now," she wrote back.

Most of them replied: "I understand. Good luck."

But one man was different. Introducing himself as John Edwin Robinson (though his real middle name was Edward) and describing himself as a divorced Kansas City businessman, he seemed to take a keen interest in the fact that she was unemployed. "Tell me a little bit more," he wrote, signing his notes JR. "How long have you been looking for work?' "

An e-mail or two later and JR was suggesting that Vickie send him her resume and come to Kansas. He said he had a lot of contacts with psychologists and psychiatrists and could help obtain her license and find work. If there was sexual chemistry, he added, he would arrange for her to move with him into his five-bedroom house and be his full-time slave. He also gave her the e-mail addresses of two references: slavedancer@hotmail.com and KCSlave@email.com.

Vickie e-mailed the references and immediately got a response from a woman named "Izzy" at the address, slavedancer@hotmail.com. "She said she was a nurse, that her husband was a doctor and that [Robinson] had helped her a lot . . . and trained her husband to be a Master," Vickie later told detectives. "She was also very quick to say that . . . he was very wealthy and did not have to work if he didn't want to and that one of the things that he had done was to help professional women get started in the area."

Izzy also mentioned that JR liked to photograph his slaves but reassured Vickie that it was only for his personal use. She went on to describe him in glowing terms. "Fifty slaves," she gushed to Vickie, "would love to be in your shoes."

That JR never provided Vickie with phone numbers so she could call his references seemed strange. But in her eagerness

For example, JR wired just $100 when he knew Vickie had to drive seven hundred miles and planned to stop at a hotel. She was grateful for any amount of money but perplexed that he didn't wire at least enough to cover her gas and stay at a decent motel. Since she thought it was to be primarily a professional encounter, she also wondered why he didn't offer to fly her. The amount was so minimal for someone seemingly so wealthy.

Then there was the issue of the slave contract, which JR e-mailed the day before her departure. Though she'd heard of them, she said this was the first time she'd ever read one and much of the language really bothered her. "I pledge my master my complete obedience and will never question his decisions or commands," it began. "I hereby offer my master my entire body to use as he wishes for his personal sexual pleasure. I beg my master to use my breasts and nipples, asshole, pussy and mouth to serve his needs. . . ."

The two-page contract included a list of twelve rules that Vickie would be required to follow, concluding with: "I offer this contract to my master of my own free will and beg my master to accept me as his personal slut, whore and slave." That last phrase was particularly loathsome to Vickie, who did not want to be anyone's "personal slut, whore and slave." She wondered if JR had any respect for her or was simply planning to use her for sex but decided to wait until she arrived in Kansas City to take the matter up with him in person.

Following JR's instructions, Vickie packed her spiked heels and a plaid bag full of her treasured sex toys, complete with whips, paddles and riding crops. On Easter Sunday, she set off in her Saturn with her Maltese, Mary Kate, arriving at Overland Park's Extended Stay America that evening, a day earlier than expected.

When the front-desk clerk found her reservation, JR hadn't paid for the room as he'd promised. She tried to call him on his cell phone. Reaching only his voice mail, she left a message for him that she'd arrived and needed to check in. After

Chapter 13

"So you arrived okay?"

JR sounded happy to hear Vickie's voice when he returned her call at eight o'clock the next morning, April 24. He told her he had been out of the country and had only returned late the night before. He assured her he would take care of the hotel bill and come to see her in an hour.

Wanting to make a good impression, she took her time getting ready, donning a loose-fitting burgundy dress that reached to her calves, taupe panty hose and black pumps. She also applied brown mascara, some soft brown eye shadow, face powder, powder blush and lipstick that matched her dress. She made a pot of coffee and waited.

At 9:30 A.M., Robinson stopped by the Extended Stay office and inquired how Vickie had paid. When he was told about the check, he asked for it back so he could pay for her entire stay through April 27. But the clerk told him that was impossible; Vickie's check had already been deposited. Upon hearing that, "Robinson became very angry," said Detective Perry Meyer, one of the detectives following him that day. "He threatened to place a stop payment."

A few minutes later, Robinson, carrying a black pilot's bag and a camera, knocked on Vickie's door. He was dressed casually, wearing blue jeans and a white dress shirt. She greeted him warmly and offered him some coffee. He said nothing about his problems with the front desk, she said, and they started off with small talk. "He was very well groomed in his own way," Vickie recalled. "He was very charismatic, and as

fessed that she wasn't ready to sign it. "Well, we can reword it if you want," said Robinson, insisting that "personal slut and whore" were affectionate, not demeaning, terms in the BDSM lexicon. They agreed upon some changes and she said she would have it ready for him later.

It was at this point that Robinson took off all his clothes and stretched himself out naked on the bed. "This is how we figure out if there's chemistry," he told her. "I want you to take your hands and rub me all over." He hugged her and told her he wanted oral sex. "I tried," she said. "He said I wasn't doing it right. That's when he pulled out a camera and he told me to look at him while I was trying to do that, and he started to take pictures."

While she had not given him permission, she didn't strongly object. "I protested, but not very much at that point," she later said. "I didn't want to do that right then because he told me that if I were going to be a good slave, that this was something that I was going to have to do and to do any less would be unsophisticated on my part."

Robinson moved from the bed to a rocking chair, pulling Vickie by the hair and forcing her to kneel before him. He continued to snap away, which she found offensive. Still gripping her hair, he grew physically excited, she said, as he thrust himself in Vickie's mouth and pulled her head back and forth until he ejaculated. Vickie gagged. "It was not enjoyable," she said. "He had wanted me to swallow it, and the taste was very, very sour, and I probably apologized for gagging."

"If I eat celery, it's going to change the taste," she said Robinson told her.

He gave Vickie about $50 for food and left the hotel about 3:00 P.M. He had handed Vickie his black pilot's bag containing sex toys, which she looked through later that day. Inside the bag were all kinds of floggers, chains, collars and leather restraints. "Even though I don't go to BDSM events very much, I had the opportunity to once go to a dungeon and I've probably seen everything that you can see," she later told de-

Robinson's response was to take off all his clothes again and sit in the rocker. Smiling, he told Vickie to do the same, but she didn't take him seriously. Then JR grew irritated and yanked off her shirt. Frightened by his aggression, Vickie took off her jeans and, following his instructions, got up on the bed on her knees.

Pulling one of the collars out of his bag, JR fastened it around Vickie's neck and tied her wrists behind her back. The collar and wrist restraints were connected by rope in such a way that Vickie would begin to choke if she moved her hands. "Owww, that's tight," she told JR. But he ignored her and kept on placing floggers and straps on the bed in front of her, as if he were about to start "playing" with her. Instead, he sat down in the rocker, with a wide grin on his face, and once again pulled out the camera. "Please stop," she pleaded as he snapped away. "I don't want you to do this." Laughing, he continued to ignore her; Vickie grew angry: "I'm going to go back to Galveston if you don't stop!"

It was JR's turn to get angry. Lowther, who had once again taken up his position in the hallway, heard him say, "I thought we got through the difficult part of this yesterday." Removing her collar, he told Vickie, "You're unsophisticated. If you were truly a slave, you would have no qualms about me taking pictures. If you want to go back: fine. If you don't, you have my number."

He put his clothes back on and packed up his toys.

Lowther, who suspected that Robinson was about to leave, started to walk back to room 122. Sure enough, he heard the door to Vickie's room suddenly open behind him. He did not run through his door and close it, fearing it would look suspicious. Instead, Lowther casually stood in the doorway while Robinson walked right by him, carrying the pilot's bag and looking down at the floor. He appeared upset.

Lowther returned to the hallway: there was no sound coming from room 120. Growing concerned for Vickie's welfare, he called her room.

He put his penis between her breasts, squeezed them together and, thrusting back and forth, quickly ejaculated. Then he asked her to rub his semen all over her body.

"Taste it now," he commanded. "Can you tell that it's sweet? It's because of the celery."

Once again, JR put the restrictive collar and wrist restraints on her and took out some wooden paddles. He didn't seem to know how to use them, Vickie thought, hitting her five or six times before switching sides. An experienced master would have alternated blows, she said, beginning softly as a warm-up and waiting for his submissive to ask for more. With JR, there was no warm-up. Suddenly he hit her so hard she screamed out in pain.

Afterward, he left Vickie lying, still tied up and facedown on the bed. Any other "player" would have come over and taken off the restraints and comforted her. Instead, JR pulled out the camera and, looking through the viewfinder, commented: "Slave resting." Once again, he began to snap away.

Then, dressing quickly, he told her he had to fly to Israel that night. He wanted her to return to Galveston to pack and promised to send a North American Van Lines truck in two weeks to move her to Kansas City. He gave her $60 for the trip home and picked up her bag of sex toys. "You don't need these," he told her. "This is one way to get you back."

Vickie drove through the night and arrived home Thursday morning, April 27. That afternoon, she began a series of e-mails to JR that his defense attorneys would later play to their full advantage. She thanked him for inviting her to Kansas and said she was excited at the prospect of moving there permanently to be with him. She also apologized for her erratic behavior. "You saw me at my absolute worst," she wrote. "The stresses of the past year have been what those in our field call 'chronic.'"

Then, she said, there were the pictures. "While I'm not a prude, I'm not used to being naked in front of someone I've just met," she wrote. "Perhaps such encounters are a facet of

SLAVE MASTER   121

call the next day to set the wheels in motion. After several
more days of waiting, Vickie gave up. She couldn't put her
life on hold any longer. She wanted to end the relationship
once and for all.

On May 11, she sent him a very stern "buzz off" e-mail that
had been crafted for her by an acquaintance in the BDSM community. She forcefully told him to keep away from her and that
she did not want to hear from him or his "references" by e-mail,
letter, telephone or in person. "I will not say or write this twice,"
she wrote. "KEEP AWAY FROM ME. If you do not abide by
what I have asked, I will contact the police and report you for
harassing me."

Her e-mail might have been the end of it all, had it not been
for the fact that JR still had Vickie's sex toys. It continued to
eat away at her that he hadn't returned them and she decided
to write once more. "The toys I had were gifts and had senti-
mental value," she pleaded on May 22. "I want nothing from
you—just to have my implements returned."

She unknowingly hit a nerve, for Robinson instantly shot
back: "If you continue to harass me, I will go to the authorities.
I will have my attorney handle any further contact by forwarding a copy of your [slave] contract to the state licensing board.
Do not contact me again, ever!"

Completely rattled by this point, Vickie wasn't about to respond. Instead, she took a different course of action—one
with ramifications she never could have imagined.

pointing meeting about wiretaps later that same day. ADA John Cowles, who was now helping Morrison and Welch with some aspects of the case, said they still weren't there yet. Then an argument ensued over whether to confront Robinson. Should they use the "dumb detective" method or hit him hard with everything they had? "Everyone was starting to show the stress," Roth said. "People were going back through the casebooks trying to see if something was missed. It had reached a point where people were looking for anything to jump-start the investigation."

On May 4, they got a small but important break when Meyer, filling in for Owsley, went through the trash and found a bill for Peoples Telecommunications, Inc., out of La Cygne, Kansas. They had no idea until that moment that he had a phone on his farm. Even more exciting was the fact that the bill showed someone placing a call to the front office of Santa Barbara Estates at 11:43 A.M. on March 1. "To us, this fit right in with the timetable we had created for that fateful day," Roth said. "It also gave us more indication that Suzette had been taken to the farm. Was the phone call to Nancy to say he'd be late for lunch?"

The following week, on May 9, as detectives began running down numbers that Robinson had called on his cell phone, they came across a man named Arthur Buschmann. It didn't take them long to figure out that the two probably met in the early 1990s when both were incarcerated at Western Missouri Correctional Center in Cameron, Missouri. Robinson had called Buschmann on numerous occasions over the years—including the periods when Izabela and Suzette went missing. Over the course of the next several days, detectives did a lot of digging into Buschmann's background, learning that he was a career crook with many convictions for forgery, burglary, drug dealing and fraud. For fear of jeopardizing the investigation, however, they held off contacting him. Interviews would have to wait.

Meanwhile, Owsley discovered two old typewritten notes in the trash that starkly illustrated how Robinson's infidelities had

call placed the next day to the same number. Was it just a co-incidence that he made the calls at the same time the cards and letters had been postmarked to the Troutens? Detectives didn't think so.

Robinson's subpoenaed American Express records sent Detectives Beyer and Dougan over to the Guesthouse Suites on May 15, 2000, to check out an old transaction for $331.52. Tim Herrman, the assistant manager, checked Robinson's name in the computer and could find no record of the charge. However, that changed when he plugged in his American Express number. The room registration card indicated that a woman named Alesia Cox had checked into room 223 on April 30, 1999, and stayed a week. The card, however, did not provide any personal information for Cox. Was she alive? They'd have to wait for the answer.

That same day, the pace of the investigation once again picked up. Robinson called the Extended Stay in Overland Park. Browning went down to talk to the clerks, who confirmed that Jeanna Milliron was expected back in town the next day. By this point, they were familiar with Robinson's habits and knew that with a woman en route he would soon pay a visit to the locker at Needmor Storage to retrieve his black pilot's bag of sex toys. Sergeant Browning had playfully dubbed his bag the "ACME Spankmaster Kit."

Detectives were still pulling out the stops trying to get a look inside the locker. Roth and Brown came up with the idea of sending Detective Dawn Layman to pose as a damsel in distress with car trouble. However, storage facility workers told them Robinson always parked his truck right in front of the locker door and had hurriedly closed it on one occasion when they approached. So instead, detectives decided to borrow a lift truck from the city, park it on the street by a power pole and station two of their men in the cherry picker. They had just gotten it all lined up when Needmor called; Robinson had already shown up. As luck would have it, too, detectives hadn't even gotten there in time to change the VHS

that Robinson had just checked Milliron into the Guesthouse Suites. Milliron, wearing a T-shirt and shorts, drove up a little while later and disappeared inside room 124. Her white Chevy Corsica, Dougan reported, was packed solid. Once again, they'd need two surveillance teams—one for Robinson and one for the lady in town. Roth arranged with O'Neal to set up the Overland Park van in the Guesthouse Suites parking lot; he stationed a couple of his own guys in the room next door. They watched as Robinson showed up at the hotel in the afternoon and stayed about an hour. The walls were thick, however, and surveillance officers couldn't hear a thing.

Meanwhile, Beyer and Bussell sat up in the cherry picker outside Robinson's Needmor Storage locker all day, the only result being a good argument with a power company official who protested loudly about them working on a city utility pole. The officers finally flashed their badges and told the official to get lost.

Robinson did not visit Milliron over the next two days, instead calling her several times from home. In the much-needed lull, Roth and his crew worked on preparing the wiretap. After a lengthy talk on Friday, May 19, 2000, he and Brown decided to ask the DA for a minimization meeting on Monday before going live with the wiretap on Tuesday. Of course, Morrison would make the final call.

Several officers were sitting in the wiretap room when the phone rang for Dougan, who quickly put the call on speakerphone. It was the clerk from the Guesthouse Suites. Milliron had just come to the front office, crying and shaking, and asked for the name of the man who had checked her in. When the clerk told her it was John Robinson, she grew hysterical.

Milliron, at the clerk's suggestion, called police a few minutes later. In response, Brown and Browning threw on police uniforms and drove to the hotel. Roth also dispatched Layman and Beyer to keep an eye on Robinson at his Monterey Lane address. They soon called to report that he had left the house, wearing a suit and tie, with Nancy. It looked as though

husband and grandpa. The plan was to bring Milliron back into the station Saturday morning, May 20, for a lengthy taped interview. Then either Monday or Tuesday, they'd have her call Robinson and ask for some money to get back home. *I hope he turns her down,* Roth thought. *It would play good for a jury.*

Brown called Roth at home the next morning to tell him Boyer was en route to pick up Milliron and bring her into the station. Brown, who planned to attend one of his kids' soccer games later that afternoon, showed up in sweatshirt and shorts. He and Boyer walked Milliron through her entire relationship with Robinson, eventually approaching the subject of sex. Milliron explained how Robinson had instructed her over the phone to strip naked and kneel by the bed until his arrival. When he discovered she'd gotten up a couple of times, she said, he struck her. That had happened during the first visit in April and again this time around.

When Brown asked her what she called Robinson, she told them she used to call him JT but that he made her switch to "master" or "sir" soon after they met. At that point, Boyer walked out of the interview and down the hall to Roth's office. He leaned over his sergeant's desk and pointed a finger in his face. "I hate Mr. Robinson," Boyer told him, "that arrogant son of a bitch."

Roth could certainly relate to Boyer's anger and disgust. The interview on Saturday morning only underscored their belief that Robinson had plans for Milliron, but not the ones she had in mind. She had given police the slave contract she had signed and allowed them to retrieve the e-mails she had exchanged with Robinson; he had all her personal and financial information. "I'm quite sure he was setting her up for the great demise," Roth said. "Milliron seemed an excellent victim that a jury, if she got there, should really find believable and feel for her. What Robinson had done to her was, to me, so damned degrading. And then when you sat and read the slave contract, you wanted to strangle him."

The next day, Barbara Sandre flew back into town. Then a

had experienced. They decided Boyer and Wilson should meet her face to face.

The next day, May 23, Wilson and Boyer found themselves driving to Little Rock, Arkansas, to intercept the psychologist, who had just left Texas and was moving to Virginia. The long drive was a good opportunity for the two detectives to get to know each other better. "Jake and I found that we had a lot of the same likes, dislikes, hobbies and think the same way about a lot of things," said Wilson. "[For example,] we both enjoy golf, the mountains and cool weather versus the heat. We are both kind of type "A" personalities. And when we were driving to Arkansas, we even learned that we got married on the exact same day. The biggest thing that came out of the drive was the respect and trust that we both garnered from the other. When I first went to Lenexa, they treated me very well but they needed to get to know me. Once they did, it was like I was one of their own."

Over the course of a four-hour interview the next afternoon, the detectives heard all about Vickie's encounter with Robinson and the graphic world of BDSM. "She had taken pretty good notes and kept copies of her emails," Wilson said. "She did want to play it off like she was completely naïve and a novice about this whole BDSM thing but it got to a point where she told us stuff in such detail that I finally told her it was apparent she was a step or two above being a novice."

Discussion about her wide array of stolen sex toys, alone, was an eye-opener for the detectives. She told them that the plaid mesh bag Robinson had stolen from her contained, among other things, a strawberry-flavored dildo worth $30 and a blue butt plug that cost $60. "Now, I'm no prude," quipped Boyer, "but I was shocked to learn that a butt plug could be worth more than a flavored dildo."

Despite the inevitable jokes, however, the detectives believed Vickie to be a very credible witness. She was articulate, intelligent and well educated—"After all, she had a Ph.D. in psychology," noted Boyer. Unlike some other women who had

Thursday, May 25, 2000, was full of important developments. Detectives opened the subpoenaed records of Specialty Publications and found that Robinson had written checks to two women. One of them, Alesia Cox, they recognized from the Guesthouse Suites registration records. But they had never heard of the second: Izabela Lewicka. As Roth flipped through the pages, he noted that Robinson had written numerous checks to Lewicka, totaling thousands of dollars, including one that was made out to Izabela Lewicka Robinson. She was obviously important to him, he realized. He came across an August 1, 1999, check in her name and then an August 23, 1999, check to a moving company called Two Men and a Truck. Turning several more pages, he saw there were no more checks to Lewicka. Roth showed the records to Brown, grimly stating: "This doesn't bode well for Izabela."

That day, saying it had gone very well, Boyer and Wilson returned from Little Rock with Neufeld's complaints of aggravated sexual battery, felony theft and blackmail against Robinson. Detectives were pumped to also pick up Lore Remington on the wiretap, capturing a conversation between her and Robinson that would be played later in court. They grew disturbed, however, when they also listened to an unidentified Tennessee woman telling him she was packed and ready. She would be traveling to Kansas City with her eight-year-old daughter the next week. "Sandre was back in town," Roth said. "Milliron was flip-flopping on us and now we had a woman bringing her eight-year-old daughter into the fray. This phone call caused unity in the police ranks. That woman and child would not meet Robinson."

Roth went to see Meier early the next morning, finally confiding in his good friend that his wife of twenty-five years was leaving him. He hadn't yet come to terms with the news himself and it wasn't an easy conversation. "Me and John went back over twenty years," Roth said. "He knew my wife very well. She took care of his two boys for a while. He was very sorry about it."

Chapter 15

Roth and his detectives had their hands full. While Brown worked with the DA's office to prepare affidavits for the search warrants, the sergeant doled out assignments: Boyer and Wilson would confront and arrest Robinson. As the designated search team, Lowther, Layman and Owsley would collect evidence at Robinson's Olathe home and storage locker. Missouri K-9 Search and Rescue, Inc., with their highly trained handlers and dogs, would have first crack at the Linn County farm. They would be joined by dozens of investigators, agents and crime scene specialists from multiple jurisdictions.

That Wednesday, Owsley went through Robinson's trash for the last time. Roth didn't know whether to laugh or cry when the detective found a note, apparently penned by their suspect, which read as follows: "Picking up peoples' trash from in front of their homes is an illegal activity!!! A videotape of you, your vehicle license plates will be turned over to the police. Have a nice day." Robinson had signed off with a smiley face. "Did he see us?" Roth asked. "Did the trashman alert him? We were never to know the answer. After a few minutes, though, we pretty much thought, 'What the hell, what can he do now?'"

Meeting on Thursday for hamburgers and grilled-chicken sandwiches at Chili's restaurant, Roth went over the final arrangements with Reed and O'Neal. Among other things, they agreed that Overland Park would safeguard the Raymore, Missouri, storage lockers through the weekend while Lenexa searched the Kansas sites. The Overland Park investigators believed the Raymore lockers—particularly the one that Nancy

vously puffing away. Then Nancy Robinson left for work. When Reed arrived shortly thereafter, they decided that Overland Park's detectives Bill Batt and Bobbi Jo Hohnholt would interview her separately from her husband. But what was keeping Brown? To their relief, he finally called at 9:30 A.M.; the judge had just signed the warrants.

Wilson hadn't eaten much all week, his stomach in knots as he contemplated what it would be like to put handcuffs on Robinson. "By this time, we had a pretty good feel for what this guy was and I just didn't want to do anything to blow it," he said. Boyer, the old-timer, was chomping at the bit: "All the hard work we had done on this case was about to pay off."

Just after 9:30 A.M., the two detectives pulled up to the Monterey Lane address and knocked on the front door of the tidy gray-and-white double-wide. Sheba, the family dog, barked loudly as Robinson, dressed in a worn T-shirt, blue jeans and slippers, answered the knock and invited them in. Walking into the living room, Wilson was struck by all the photos on the wall. "There he was with the kids, with the grandkids, growing up through the ages," he recalled. "As I thought of my daughter and the way she loves her grandpa, I couldn't help but wonder what this was going to do to his family. To this day I feel sad for them."

The detectives, wearing dark suits, sat opposite Robinson, who sank into a recliner near the door. "We want to visit with you a little bit," said Wilson, handing him his card as Boyer quickly got down to business and explained that they were responding to complaints from Vickie Neufeld and Jeanna Milliron. Turning beet red, Robinson acknowledged that he had engaged in BDSM sessions with the women. But he insisted that they were consensual and the rest was a misunderstanding. He was happy to return Vickie's sex toys if she would send him postage. He had never tried to blackmail either one of them, insisting he had destroyed their photos. He also denied telling Milliron his name was Jim or James Turner or that he had ever used that name with anyone. "Why would I do that?" he asked.

tening to John Robinson lie to them, like he had done to so many other people. Having heard more than enough, he told him they would like him to come down to the station and give a statement. Robinson stalled, saying he wanted to change his clothes and shave first. "I want to keep my wife out of this," he added. "She has no idea about the lifestyle. This is compromising a thirty-six-year marriage."

Suddenly Robinson jumped up, saying he needed to call his lawyer. At this point, the detectives moved in to block him from getting anywhere near his computers and told him he was under arrest. "What for?" Robinson asked. Sexual battery, blackmail and theft, Boyer told him.

Robinson appeared surprised but sat quietly. Boyer, on the other hand, started pacing the floor like a caged tiger. "I was going over the case in my head and thinking of all of the women that Robinson had conned, stolen from and probably murdered," he said. "I thought how much I despised this man for the way he treated these women."

As he continued to pace back and forth, Boyer told his prisoner, "Don't be surprised if we charge you with murder." Robinson, with a confused look on his face, leaned forward in his chair and asked, "Murder?"

"Yes, murder," Boyer replied. "Five counts."

The veteran detective started rattling off the names: Suzette Trouten, Paula Godfrey, Catherine Clampitt, Lisa and Tiffany Stasi. At the mention of Suzette, Robinson fell back in his chair and all the color left his face. At Lisa and Tiffany, he took off his glasses, wiped his brow, glanced at Wilson and muttered, "Jesus Christ."

"You could see him kind of crumble in this recliner that he was sitting in," Wilson remembered. "He was hyperventilating and he kept taking his glasses off and wiping his brow. The guy was imploding."

After placing him in handcuffs, the detectives led Robinson out through the screened-in porch attached to his trailer home. By this time, police were pulling up in unmarked cars and

Chapter 16

As soon as Robinson was escorted to a waiting police car, the designated search team—Dawn Layman, Dan Owsley and Mike Lowther—moved into the Monterey double-wide and got down to work. "We didn't expect to find much at his home, but we were wrong," Roth said. In fact, there was a treasure trove of incriminating evidence. "We started finding stuff right away," agreed Lowther. "Every five seconds, it was like, 'Hey, come look at this' or 'Oh my God, look what I found.'"

Specialty Publications checks were lying out on the kitchen table. The master bedroom yielded a collection of eighteen adult videos. A second bedroom had been converted into an office that Robinson shared with his wife and—after three desktop computers, two laptops, a printer and a fax machine had been hauled away for examination by forensic experts—the search team found files dating back years. Unbelievably, an expandable folder in the closet contained the 1985 receipt for Lisa Stasi's stay at the Rodeway Inn, as well as a single blank piece of paper bearing her signature and an envelope addressed to Stasi's brother.

Also in the closet inside a black soft-sided briefcase was a checkbook containing the names of account holders Barbara L. Sandre and John Robinson, Social Security benefit statements from 1999 for a Debbie L. Faith and Sheila D. Faith and pieces of paper with e-mail addresses scribbled all over them. Several were eerily familiar to detectives: midwestmaster, eruditemaster, preipo, slavedancer and KCslave.

The black soft-sided bag also contained Robinson's passport,

Robinson. Under *B,* they found listings for Beverly Bonner and BJB. Both names had been crossed out with a big X.

While the search team was processing Robinson's home, Overland Park detectives Bobbi Jo Hohnholt and Bill Batt had gone to the Santa Barbara Estates front office to speak to Nancy. When asked if there was a quiet place where they could talk, she suggested they step outside. Out in the parking lot, they informed her that her husband had just been arrested for sexual battery, blackmail and felony theft. The petite blond-haired woman clutched her chest. "I can't believe my husband would do something like that," she answered, gasping.

Nancy agreed to accompany the detectives back to the Overland Park police station for a lengthy taped interview. According to police records, the detectives informed her on the way over that her husband had run up more than $50,000 in charges on just one of his credit cards. Visibly blanching, she told them she would be in a coma if she had known they were in that much debt.

Robinson's wife told the detectives that her husband had been consumed with the Internet ever since he bought his first computer several years earlier. She acknowledged that she was aware of his interest in BDSM, but she couldn't comprehend it. From time to time, she noted that he left BDSM "material" lying around, but she refused to read any of it or view his collection of sadomasochistic sex tapes.

She also admitted she had recently found out about Barbara Sandre and had driven by her address Grant Avenue. She knew her husband had an affair with Sandre in the 1970s but had had no idea how they had recently become reacquainted; she was getting ready to confront him once again. "Guess that makes me feel really silly!" Nancy exclaimed to detectives. "When did that woman move back to Grant?"

Though she would later acknowledge knowing more, Nancy told detectives she knew "Iza," "byza" or "Izzy" Lewicka to be her husband's friend who had done work on his manufactured modular home magazine. Questioned about

Neufeld, more Social Security benefit statements for Sheila D. Faith and Debbie L. Faith, and two 1997 Social Security checks, for $582 each, made out in their names.

Layman opened a brown leather briefcase that contained a number of Suzette's personal effects, including her Michigan driver's license, Social Security card, birth certificate and application for a passport. It also held forty-two preaddressed envelopes to various members of the Trouten family and thirty-one sheets of pastel colored stationery, blank except for the signature "Love ya, Suzette." There was also her yellow legal pad listing the names and home and e-mail addresses of friends and family, her slave contract containing 128 rules and an unlabeled videocassette.

In a black pilot's bag—the one that Robinson carried with him when he met the various women coming into town —were a variety of floggers, pieces of rope, clothespins, several golf balls and the harness he had used on Vickie. A blue nylon bag with black handles in the locker contained several nude photos of Suzette, as well as a number of her sex toys, including a collar, dildos, butt plugs and a metal speculum, electrodes and a battery-powered electrical device called a TENS unit. Recovered from a Hyvee grocery bag was Suzette's journal. In the various cardboard boxes were many of her knickknacks, jewelry and anatomy and physiology textbooks. "There was just a ton of stuff," Lowther said.

After several hours, they transported all of the property to the Lenexa Police Department, where Morrison, Welch and Cowles joined them. "Everyone was excited with the results of the two searches," Roth remembered. "[The detectives] worked well into the night and still hadn't finished booking property." It was past midnight when the last detectives, tired but pleased, headed home for some much-deserved rest. Saturday morning would be the farm.

see initially was a Big Boy box matching the ones Suzette had brought with her from Michigan."

Besides killing a snake with a shovel, in fact, Roth felt as though the entire morning was a disappointment. The K-9 teams worked east to a collapsed building and a nearby concrete foundation, then south to the pond near the back of the property. Once they had cleared the area, Overland Park's five-member underwater team began a hand search of the snake-infested pond, looking for bodies, weapons, clothes or anything else that might point to evidence of foul play.

The rest of the investigators began combing other areas of the farm, including a jumble of metal and plastic barrels and lawn equipment in undergrowth next to the shed. By lunchtime, they had covered a lot of ground but had little to show for their efforts. "It was very hot and humid, the chiggers were in legions and I, for one, was rather glum when we broke for lunch," Roth said. "So far, we had found nothing in the trailer that stood out and nothing remotely close to a grave site."

Lenexa had done a good job of planning ahead in the eating department, however, packing grills, chips and coolers filled with hamburgers, hot dogs, soda and bottled water. While Roth was munching on a freshly grilled hamburger, K-9 handler Petra Stephens approached and asked if he could have someone move some barrels away from a small shed that stood a stone's throw from the trailer. One of her Border Collies, Wolf, had shown some interest, she added, but there was so much other junk in the way she couldn't get them in there for a good sniff. "Since I'd seen the handlers down there earlier actually leaning on the barrels, I didn't give the finding much hope," Roth remembered.

Strolling to the shed a few minutes later, he found Stephens working her collie around two yellow eighty-five-gallon metal drums. By this point, she had also removed the small plug from the top of one of the barrels and reported that it "smelled kind of bad." Roth threw a few items out of the way and began rocking one of the yellow drums from side to side

Robinson to justice." They had hoped to find Suzette and were already convinced she was Unknown No. 1, but the discovery of a second body came as something of a shock. "It immediately reinforced the belief that we were dealing with a serial killer," Reed said. "It also raised the question: exactly how many more victims were we going to find?

While Assistant District Attorney Sara Welch spent her Sunday at the courthouse in Cass County, Missouri, securing the search warrant for Robinson's Raymore storage locker, Dr. Donald Pojman spent his at the Shawnee County Coroner's Office in Topeka, Kansas, performing autopsies on Unknown No. 1 and Unknown No. 2. After an all-day session observed by Detectives Hohnholt and Boyer, who took careful notes, the deputy coroner concluded that both were females who had been viciously bludgeoned to death by a weapon consistent with a hammer.

Unknown No. 1 had died instantly after being dealt a single blow to the left side of the head that left a quarter-size hole in her skull. She wore nothing but a black cloth blindfold that appeared to be held in place by a soft nylon rope encircling her face and neck; the only other article in the barrel was a plastic Price Chopper bag. Her long hair had been pulled back into a ponytail and she had several piercings in her ears, nipples and genitalia. Mildly decomposed, she had been dead a few months to a year. Using dental records, a forensic odontologist would soon confirm what detectives already knew in their hearts. Unknown No. 1 was Suzette Trouten.

A turquoise diamond-shaped patterned pillow partially covered Unknown No. 2, who was wearing a dark short-sleeve nightshirt. Three pieces of gray duct tape, found floating loose in the barrel, could have been used to bind or muzzle her. Bludgeoned twice on the left side of the head—and judging by the blood that had collected in the subdural region of the brain—she may have lived fifteen minutes. Moderately decomposed, she had been dead for six months to two years. It would take a week to obtain the dental records

Chapter 18

Roth and Reed hadn't even left the Linn County crime scene on Saturday afternoon, when, sitting in a police cruiser, they decided it would be a good idea to form an official joint task force to continue their investigation, as it undoubtedly was about to send them in countless directions. The next day, Sunday, June 4, 2000, they met with their respective chiefs, who put Captain Meier in charge and appointed Reed as the lead officer and Roth as the report officer. The task force, it was determined, would be jointly controlled by Lenexa and Overland Park but continue to operate out of Lenexa.

Lenexa's technicians worked feverishly over the weekend transforming the large police classroom on the station's top floor into the new task force headquarters. Phone and power lines dropped from the ceiling tiles and four computers—to be used for entering police reports—were stationed in the middle of the room. Long tables were banked around the computers and phones with recorders were positioned every few chairs.

As the room started to fill on Monday morning, June 5, the makeup of the group now working the case took on a new look. Investigators from Linn County and the Kansas Bureau of Investigation joined the Lenexa and Overland Park detectives. Though technically not on the task force, members of the Directed Patrol Unit were also there, along with a few detectives who had been sent back to work the daily cases. There were also seats for Morrison, Welch and Cowles from the DA's office, Lenexa's chief Ellen Hanson and other important guests.

The biggest change, however, was that the lead investigators

their way to the back of the locker. After about ten minutes, Lowther heard someone say, "Are those barrels under there?"

Sure enough, in the rear left corner, they could barely make out a black metal barrel standing by itself and two blue metal barrels that appeared to be covered by a heavy opaque plastic tarp. Newspapers, a crib mattress, a dog carrier and a brown tent were stacked on top of the barrels in an apparent effort to hide them from view.

Removing the items, they realized that the blue barrels were not only covered in heavy plastic but also individually wrapped in plastic and secured with copious amounts of gray duct tape. A bag of gray kitty litter had been spread on the floor around the blue barrels to soak up fluid that was leaking from them.

At this point, Kevin Winer, an evidence technician from the Kansas City, Missouri, Crime Lab, was called to the scene. He decided to open the black barrel, which was sitting by itself in a back corner with the words "rendered pork fat" on the label. Looking inside, investigators saw an amorphous mass halfway filling the barrel. Winer grabbed a stick and began poking around in the barrel, identifying a brown sheet, a pair of glasses and some dark shoes. He lifted up one of the shoes. There was a leg attached.

No sooner had the newly formed task force begun to chase the leads they had sat on for weeks when Lowther called about 10:30 A.M. from Raymore, Missouri, to report the discovery of the three barrels in Robinson's storage locker. " 'Now we might have to switch gears,' " Roth remembered thinking upon hearing the news. "Although they hadn't opened the barrels, he said there was kitty litter and a bad smell. We knew our case had just escalated."

Reed and Roth, who were supposed to be running the day-to-day operations, instead spent the first day just trying to keep up with the phones. Lowther called back a little later and confirmed that one barrel had been opened at the scene and it did, indeed, contain a body. Raymore investigators were buying three plastic wading pools to set the barrels in, since

that Robinson had stolen more than $700 worth of whips, paddles, riding crops and other sex toys.

Morrison told reporters that Robinson allegedly had used the Internet to develop relationships with these and other women interested in sadomasochism. He was apparently known to use the screen name "slavemaster" in his computer correspondence and sometimes called himself James Turner in person, he reportedly said. "This case has to do with the suspect having numerous contacts throughout the United States who share similar interests over, among other things, the Internet," Morrison said.

(Forensic experts analyzing Robinson's computers would later determine he never actually used the "slavemaster" handle, but the media immediately seized on the apt and catchy description and, not surprisingly, it stuck.)

Stites also said that about twenty investigators, including some from the FBI and the Kansas Bureau of Investigation, were continuing to search Robinson's farm in rural Linn County. "We are ground searching every bit of land involved and there is also a pond involved," said the laid-back country sheriff as he stepped up to the podium. "There's a possibility that we may drain that pond."

Shortly after the press conference, Robinson was led into the Johnson County Courthouse to face charges of aggravated sexual battery and felony theft. Wearing a prison standard-issue orange jumpsuit, he tried to shield himself from a barrage of waiting photographers by holding a large manila envelope over his face.

Robinson asked for a court-appointed attorney and District Judge William Cleaver appointed the public defender's office to represent him. Ted Baird, one of Morrison's assistant district attorneys, told Cleaver that prosecutors considered Robinson an extreme flight risk with previous felony convictions for theft, stealing and fraud. By the end of the hearing, the judge had increased the $250,000 bond set in his arrest warrant to $5 million—the largest in county history.

In the third barrel was the body of an overweight teenager who was dressed in a pair of green ribbed knit pants and a green knit pullover blouse. She was wearing an adult disposable diaper and, in what was left of her straight brown hair, a silver-colored barrette. She, too, had been bludgeoned several times on the back and right side of her head.

On Tuesday morning, June 6, 2000, Kansas City residents awoke to the news that a brazen serial killer had likely been operating in their very midst. POLICE NAME SUSPECT IN DEATHS OF WOMEN," blared the headline in *The Kansas City Star*, which would devote many front-page stories to the barrel murders in the coming weeks, months and years. While the *Star* focused on the two bodies found on Robinson's farm, it also mentioned that police in Raymore, Missouri, had found three suspicious fifty-five-gallon drums in Robinson's Stor-Mor For Less storage locker. After looking inside one of them, they had sent all three barrels and other evidence to the Jackson County Medical Examiner's Office and the Kansas City, Missouri, Crime Lab for analysis, Police Chief Kris Turnbow said. While Turnbow refused to divulge what police had seen in the barrel, the paper noted that Cass County prosecutor Christopher Koster had scheduled a news conference for 1:30 P.M.

The *Olathe Daily News*, the paper of record for Robinson's suburban community, reported the same day that the suspect known online as "the Slavemaster" was believed to be involved in sadomasochistic activity over the Internet and would soon be charged with murdering at least two women found on his farm. By this time, too, Kansas City's four main TV stations were all over the story, bringing its viewers the latest developments in the case. It was the biggest news to hit Kansas City in years and the media's appetite for details was insatiable.

Thanks to the trove of paperwork found in Robinson's Olathe storage locker and his home office, Roth and a handful of those detectives most familiar with the case files were pretty sure they knew just who was in the barrels. But since they hadn't yet been positively identified, police had to keep

daughter, Kim, was born—he wrote again and told her he wanted to get engaged. However, Sandre had just gotten married to her first husband and declined his proposal. She did not hear from him again for several years.

In 1969, Robinson somehow got her telephone number, she said, and called her out of the blue in Toronto. They occasionally spoke on the phone after that and in 1971 he flew to Toronto on business. She met with him and the relationship turned romantic; she even introduced him to her mother. Then Robinson left Canada, telling her he would not be able to contact her for a few months. During that time, she moved to Germany, she said. She did not hear from him for more than twenty years.

The next contact came in July 1993, she told Brown, when her mother received a letter addressed to Barbara that had purportedly been written by John Robinson's adopted son. Barbara's mother forwarded the letter to her daughter in London, where she was now living with her third husband. "Henry Robinson" explained that John Robinson was his biological uncle who had taken him and his three siblings under his wing after his father and mother had been killed in a car accident. Henry described him as a good father who never missed any of the kids' sporting events or school activities.

Now that they had grown and established themselves, Henry explained that he and his sisters and brother wanted to write the letter to Sandre as a favor to Robinson. He said that his adoptive father still carried Barbara's photograph in his wallet and cared for her. He also said that Robinson frequently spoke about her and that he and his siblings thought it would be nice if the two of them could talk again.

Barbara told Brown that at the time she and her parents were not suspicious of the typewritten letter and felt that it was genuine. Writing back to the address that had been included, Barbara once again started a correspondence with Robinson. This time, they stayed in touch by mail and by telephone. In the summer of 1994, Barbara returned to Canada,

ber of smaller items a little at a time, saying he bought them at estate sales or that they belonged to his grandmother and had been kept in storage.

At the time of Brown's call to Barbara in June 2000, Robinson had recently told her he was handing in his resignation to the CIA and their lives were in danger as a terrorist group had recently tried to kill him by planting a bomb in his car. She was in Canada hunting for a place for them to live, she said, and Robinson was supposed to follow her up there at the end of the month.

Brown was blown away by the magnitude of Robinson's lies to Barbara. "That was a tough conversation," he acknowledged. "I felt really bad telling this woman that the person she planned to live the rest of her life with was nothing but a fraud—and very likely a murderer. She was stunned, truly stunned."

Over the ensuing weeks, Brown would speak to Sandre many more times over the phone. He and his new task force partner, Bobbi Jo Hohnholt, would conduct a lengthy interview with her in person when she came back into town. By the end of their first conversation on June 6, 2000, however, Barbara had agreed to let detectives search her apartment on Grant Avenue. All they needed was for her to sign and return a form giving them her consent. What they would ultimately find there would prove to be almost as valuable as her shocking testimony.

Meanwhile, Hohnholt was chasing down a separate lead of her own. From Robinson's storage locker, detectives had recovered numerous pieces of identification belonging to Izabela Lewicka, including her passport and high school diploma. By 10:30 A.M. Tuesday, June 6, 2000, the Overland Park detective was on the phone to the West Lafayette, Indiana, Police Department, where she asked a detective if they had a missing persons report on file for the young woman. While the answer was no, the Indiana detective ran a check and found that she had surrendered her driver's license to Kansas in September

Chapter 19

Leads continued to pour into the task force. One of the first was a tip from a local couple who recognized Robinson from the news and wanted to report that he was renting a post office box from them at their Olathe mail facility. Greg Wilson and Rick Dougan were assigned to investigate, and on the morning of June 6, they headed over to the Mailroom on East Santa Fe Street, which was just down the road from the Johnson County Courthouse and not far from Robinson's home on Monterey Lane.

Randy Davis, the owner of the Mailroom, explained to the detectives that he and his wife had been watching the news coverage of the homicide investigation when they saw the suspect on television. Both immediately recognized him as a six-year customer they knew as James A. Turner. He also said that Robinson had been picking up what he believed to be Social Security benefit checks in the names of Sheila D. Faith and Debbie L. Faith since June 1994. In fact, they mentioned that two checks had arrived the Friday before—the day of Robinson's arrest—and were still sitting in box 215.

Colleen Davis, Randy's wife, told the detectives she thought it was strange that Turner always arrived to collect the checks and had asked him once where the Faith women were. Out of the country, she was told. She was pretty certain he mentioned Australia. Dougan excitedly phoned Welch and requested a search warrant.

Up to that point, Wilson said, detectives had been very puzzled as to where Robinson was getting the money to bring all

belongings to a storage locker in Raymore, Missouri. As part
of his settlement, moreover, the doctor said he had mailed a
number of $1,000 checks to his ex-wife at a post office box
in Olathe, Kansas. Back at Lenexa, Beyer quickly ran Beverly's Social Security number, which he had obtained from
her driver's license, through TransUnion. The credit-report-
ing agency spit out three previous addresses for the missing
woman. The last one: East Santa Fe Street, Olathe, Kansas.

Beyer, who was aware that similar checks for the Faith
women at the same address had been found in Robinson's
Needmor Storage locker, knew right away that something was
up. "The mail drop in Olathe had been a common denomina-
tor in this case," he said. "[Dr. Bonner] also told us that
Beverly had hired a moving company to move all of [her]
property to a storage locker in Raymore. When Jimmy told
me that . . . I pretty much knew at that point that Beverly was
going to be one of the bodies in the barrels."

That same afternoon, June 6, a joint press conference with
Chris Koster and Paul Morrison was taking place at the Cass
County Courthouse in Harrisonville, Missouri, where it was obvious (in hindsight, anyway) that detectives were staying several
steps ahead of the news. Koster confirmed that the three barrels in Robinson's Raymore storage locker had each held a
female body. He added that the badly decomposed remains had
probably been in the barrels for several years. Though they did
not reveal their cause of death, the prosecutors also confirmed
that all five victims—the two in Linn County and the three in
Cass County—had suffered severe blows to the head.

Because investigators were dealing with victims who may
have met Robinson on the Internet, the investigation
promised to be vast and laborious, Morrison said. Detectives were busy gathering and sifting through hundreds of
pieces of evidence, including pictures and names of people
Robinson corresponded with online. "In some cases, we have
names but no photographs and in others we have photographs
but no names," explained the Johnson County prosecutor.

Paula Godfrey and Catherine Clampitt, both of Overland
Park, who had vanished after going to work for him in 1984
and 1987, respectively. Morrison also said that Izabela
Lewicka, a Polish immigrant who had dated and worked for
the suspect until 1999, could not be found. Morrison admitted that one of the bodies in the barrels might be Lewicka,
who had originally been living around the Westport neighborhood of Kansas City. "This is one of those cases that
continues to unfold every day and I think it's impossible for
anyone to speculate where it will end," the prosecutor said.

   The district attorney also told reporters that police did not
believe the bodies in the Raymore barrels were those of the
missing women from the 1980s. "We're talking about a guy
here who has lived in a lot of different places and has had a
lot of contacts," he said, refusing to elaborate further. What
he didn't say was that at least two of the three women found
in the Raymore lockers were physically much heavier than
Godfrey, Stasi or Clampitt.

   Overland Park Captain Jeffrey Dysart explained to the
press that in the 1980s Robinson was presenting himself as a
businessman and philanthropist who wanted to help unwed
mothers and other young women who needed a hand. "It ap-
pears as if all these women [Godfrey, Stasi and Clampitt]
were just getting started in their lives," Dysart said. Morrison
added that the Overland Park police had worked hard to solve
the old cases but never gathered enough information to
charge Robinson with a crime. They had reopened their investigation in March 2000, he noted, when Trouten vanished
after telling relatives she had met him on the Internet and was
moving to Kansas City for a job.

   Lead No. 164 had come in at 10:52 A.M., June 7. Morrison's assistant, Terri Issa, reported to Roth that she'd received
an anonymous phone tip from a caller—identified by sources
as a close relative of Robinson's wife, Nancy—who said the
suspect had helped his brother and sister-in-law Don and
Frieda Robinson adopt a baby back in the 1980s. But as this

Robinson meant he had fired her. He emphatically denied having any knowledge of Robinson killing anyone or helping him to dispose of any bodies.

Roth was somewhat reticent when it came to talking about Buschmann, who would die in custody of natural causes. He acknowledged that the police had asked the Johnson County Crime Lab to go over the Hyundai, which they were easily able to recover since Buschmann had sold it to an acquaintance. "We went after Art real hard," Roth said. "We really thought he was going to be involved somehow. Although we had our eyes on him, none of it ever panned out." In the final analysis, the sergeant said, Buschmann was nothing more than "a lifelong crook who got rid of [Izabela's] car."

While Browning was interviewing Buschmann, Bill Batt and Mike Bussell drove down to Jenks, Oklahoma, to talk to Nancy Robinson, who was hiding out at her son's house in order to escape the press hordes that had descended upon her home in Santa Barbara Estates. According to police records, John junior first met the detectives by himself at the local Arby's, telling them that he had talked with his father shortly after his arrest. "I got involved with some really bad people," he said his father told him. "You don't know how really bad they are. I'm fucked!"

He also told police that from what he had heard on the news and from what his mother told him, there was not much doubt in his mind that his father had committed several of the murders. The question both he and his mother had, he said, was whether Robinson had acted alone. He also said that if push came to shove, he thought his father would confess the truth about what he had done, if he had killed people and where the remains were.

John junior also told the detectives that the man suspected of such heinous crimes was not the father he knew. When he was growing up, he recounted, he had been spanked when he did wrong but was never physically abused. According to what John Jr. told police, his father had not been so lucky. On

Nancy also said she was not aware that her husband was receiving any Social Security checks from Sheila or Debbie Faith. "Who are these people anyway?" she asked. When told that her husband was believed to have cashed numerous checks over the last several years, she countered, "What has he done with this money?" The detectives reportedly told her they had no idea, unless he had spent it on other women.

Batt and Bussell also showed Nancy pictures of several women, some of whom she could identify. But others, such as Neufeld and Milliron, she did not recognize. "Who are these women anyway?" she reportedly asked. "John has basically no self-esteem. I don't know why he was looking for women with less self-esteem than him."

Upon further questioning, Nancy said she wasn't familiar with Mark Boothroyd but acknowledged that her husband had met Arthur Buschmann in prison. She commented that she didn't think they were still in touch. "I told him to stay away from [Buschmann]," she said. "He is nothing but bad news."

That same afternoon, the family released their first public statement about the "surreal events" that had overwhelmed them since Robinson's arrest. "We, as a family, have followed the events of the last week in horror and dismay along with each of you," they said in a written statement, which Overland Park attorney Kelly Ryan, who was acting as the family's spokesperson, read at a news conference. "While we do not discount the information that has and continues to come to light, we do not know the person whom we have read about and heard about on TV."

The family described Robinson as a "loving and caring husband and father, the type of parent who has never missed a sporting event, a school function, or missed an opportunity to be there with his family. We have never seen any behavior that would have led us to believe that anything we are now hearing could be possible."

They also criticized what they said was the "utterly irresponsible" behavior of the news media and asked that their

were involved in any crimes. "We continue to believe that he's operating alone," he told reporters.

Morrison also said the crimes had possibly been connected to a moneymaking venture that he would not describe. One of the difficulties prosecutors faced, Morrison noted, was that Robinson had been connected to numerous businesses—at least some of them sham operations—over the years. "This case has a lot of angles," he said. "There's a sex angle; there's an Internet angle; there's also a developing financial angle that ultimately will be a very large part of this case."

Stites, for his part, said investigators had finished looking through the pond, which they had drained, and checking under the trailer on Robinson's property. They had also dug up parts of the farm in places where it looked as though the ground had been disturbed, under brush piles and around spots where dogs indicated something might be buried. They had made "no major discoveries," he concluded. That night they planned to search the barn with luminol, a substance that makes blood spots glow under a special light. They had already conducted the same process on Robinson's rural trailer.

On Friday, June 9, 2000, Johnson County judge John Anderson III—the son of a former Kansas governor, he was assigned to hear the sexual assault case pending against Robinson—met in his chambers with Morrison and regional defender Byron Cerrillo before issuing a gag order. The court also received Robinson's signed affidavit showing that he qualified for a court-appointed attorney. According to the affidavit, the suspect had been unemployed for at least the past twelve months and received $1,021 a month in Social Security benefits. It also stated that he owned land valued at $28,000, later identified as his Linn County farm.

On the same day, Brown received the consent-to-search form from Barbara Sandre, but when the detective was busy with another assignment, Roth sent Layman, Wilson and Ron Frazier to complete the investigation of Grant Avenue. Inside, they found a number of items that provided further evidence

That same evening, having just received word from the Jackson County medical examiner that one of the bodies in the Raymore storage locker had been positively identified as Beverly Bonner, Alan Beyer, called Lowell Heath, Bonner's older brother, in Mississippi. The detective gently broke the news, saying the identification had been made using dental records. Beyer asked him if he should contact the other family members. The brokenhearted Heath replied that he would prefer to notify them himself.

Paula Godfrey disappeared from Overland Park, Kansas, in August 1984. *(Courtesy of Lenexa Police Department)*

Lisa Stasi and her four-month-old daughter vanished in January 1985. *(Courtesy of Lenexa Police Department)*

Sheila Dale Faith took her 15-year-old wheelchair-bound daughter, Debbie Lynn, on vacation in the summer of 1994 from their home in Pueblo, Colorado, never to return.
(Courtesy of Lenexa Police Department)

Debbie Lynn Faith (left) with her best friend Suzanne Lawrence at their 1993 graduation from Nicolas Junior High School in Fullerton, California.
(Courtesy of Deborah Lawrence)

Robinson grew up in this nondescript home in the working-class
Chicago suburb of Cicero. *(Author's photo)*

As a 13-year-old,
Robinson met
actress
Judy Garland
backstage at the
London Palladium.
*(Courtesy of
Chicago Tribune)*

Surrounded by family in January 1985, Robinson holds four-month-old Tiffany Lynn Stasi on his lap. He was later convicted of murdering Tiffany's mother and arranging the baby's fake adoption to his unsuspecting brother. *(Courtesy of Lenexa Police Department)*

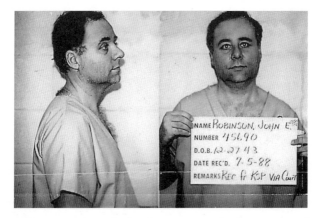

Robinson served time for fraud at Kansas Hutchinson Correctional Facility in the late 1980s. *(Courtesy of Kansas Department of Corrections)*

The investigators from the Overland Park Police Department assigned
to the Robinson case. Front row, from left: Det. Bobbi Jo Hohnholt,
Det. Jose Carrillo, Det. Ron Frazier. Back row,
from left: Det. Scott Weiler, Sgt. Joe Reed, Det. Greg Wilson,
Det. Mike Jacobson and Capt. Keith O'Neal. *(Author's photo)*

Liberty, Missouri,
probation supervisor
Stephen Haymes
suspected Robinson
as early as 1985
and aided detectives
when they reopened the
investigation in 2000.
*(Courtesy of Jim Barcus/
The Kansas City Star)*

After a sadomasochistic encounter with Robinson, Vickie Neufeld accused him of aggravated sexual battery and felony theft and testified against him at his 2002 trial. *(Courtesy of Mark Fisher)*

At the time of his arrest in June 2000, Robinson lived with his wife in this trailer at 36 Monterey Lane in Olathe, Kansas. *(Author's photo)*

Aerial view of Robinson's 16.5-acre La Cygne, Kansas, property, where authorities discovered the bludgeoned bodies of Trouten and Lewicka. *(Courtesy of Shane Keyser/The Kansas City Star)*

The twin yellow barrels on Robinson's rural property contained the bodies of Trouten and Lewicka. *(Courtesy of Lenexa Police Department)*

Investigators theorized Lewicka was murdered in her apartment in Olathe, Kansas. *(Author's photo)*

The first day of Robinson's preliminary hearing, February 5, 2001. He would later fire his defense team, from left, Ron Evans, Mark Manna and Alice Craig White. *(Courtesy of Jeff Roberson/The Kansas City Star)*

Besides the local press, the "Slavemaster" serial killer story was all over the Associated Press wires and heavyweights such as the *New York Times, USA Today,* and *Time* magazine were weighing in. Soon they would by joined by television news-magazines *Primetime* and *Dateline,* each eager to provide a unique angle. Several of them agreed with *USA Today*'s assessment on June 9, that, should Robinson be charged and convicted in the killings, "he would prove to be one of the worst murderers in state history and the first documented serial killer in the nation to use the Internet to recruit potential victims."

The media attention was overwhelming to the investigators, who had their hands full just trying to do their jobs. On Saturday morning, June 10, several of the task force supervisors—Morrison, Welch, Cowles, Meier, Roth, Reed and Brown—met behind closed doors to discuss how to stop the leaks. With the recent development out of Chicago, there was even more cause for concern. "We were worried about it leaking to the press before we could investigate," said Roth. "The Robinsons were cooperating with the FBI up there and the last thing we wanted were a bunch of reporters camped out on their doorstep."

Roth said the group suspected they knew who was dishing to the media. While the sergeant declined to elaborate, other sources in the investigation pointed to Christopher Koster, the young and enthusiastic prosecutor from Missouri who had a reputation among the local media for being a publicity hound. The supervisors questioned why they even needed to continue the task force, since Robinson was already in jail, the identification of bodies would soon be complete and murder charges forthcoming. While they didn't set a date, they agreed that the investigation would soon be restricted to Lenexa and Overland Park. "The work was slowing," Roth said. "It would seem the perfect time to disband."

Their concern was only reinforced by an article in the *Star* that day, which mentioned that police were investigating the 1994 disappearance of Beverly Bonner, a former Cameron,

women and a baby who had gone missing, as well as Robinson's frighteningly abusive relationship with Theresa Williams. Finally it noted that Beverly Bonner had disappeared after telling friends she had a wonderful job lined up, one that involved foreign travel.

The next day, June 12, Koster officially announced that Beverly Bonner was among the victims found in Robinson's Raymore locker. He acknowledged that her identity had been confirmed late Friday, using dental records, and said he had spent more than an hour talking by telephone to her relatives about the case. "Her family is obviously grief-stricken," Koster told the *Star*. "They still had hope in their hearts it might come to a better ending."

By this point, Hohnholt was getting ready to deliver some bad news to Izabela's family in Indiana. She had received a faxed report from Dr. Daniel Winter that said he had compared the dental records sent by Izabela's father with those of the body in the barrel marked Unknown No. 2. There was a match. The deceased was, in fact, Izabela Lewicka.

Hohnholt said she found it "very difficult" to call Izabela's father to break the news. "That was the hardest thing I had to do in the investigation," she said. "To do it by phone, rather than in person, makes it even worse. You keep thinking, how would you want your parents to find out?" Lewicki took his daughter's death as well as could be expected under the circumstances. "He expressed guilt over not doing more to locate his daughter," Hohnholt said. "I think he felt like they were part of the scam and he was ashamed they never recognized it."

tered letter saying he would seek the death penalty. To support his execution request, Koster said he intended to prove Robinson had committed multiple murders to receive money or something of value from his victims; and that the murders were committed in a manner outrageously or wantonly vile, horrible or inhuman, involving torture or depravity of mind.

Morrison and Koster agreed that the case would first be handled in Johnson County, where the investigation had originated and where Robinson had been held under a $5 million bond for the sexual assault and theft charges involving the two Texas women.

Koster also said he would pursue the death penalty in Missouri, even if Robinson was sentenced to die in Kansas. The families of victims found in Cass County had the right to see separate convictions for the murders of their loved ones, he said. "Unquestionably, even if the death penalty is successfully prosecuted in Kansas, we will transfer him back," he told reporters.

Returning to the task force headquarters after the news conference, Roth received a call from FBI's Tarpley, who excitedly told him he'd probably want to put him on speakerphone. Roth replied that he'd prefer to hear what he had to say first—and was soon glad he had been cautious. Tarpley told him that one of the agents in Chicago had just been talking to the attorney for Robinson's brother and sister-in-law Don and Frieda Robinson. As the agent was leaving the office, the couple had shown up and she was invited back in and given the scoop.

The couple had been trying to adopt for several years. At a family reunion in 1983, his brother in Kansas City had told them he might be able to help. After a couple of attempts, where things didn't work out, Robinson called in January 1985 to tell them he had found a baby. They immediately flew to Kansas City, stopping by his office at Equi-II to sign the paperwork. Robinson had also said his attorney Doug Wood was handling the private adoption and they saw that Wood's

ing the first sketchy details about Sheila and Debbie Faith. Kathy Norman, who was one of Sheila's two sisters, said they had last spoken in 1994. Sheila had lived in California with her daughter for many years but moved to Colorado not long after her husband had died in 1991. While in Colorado, Sheila told Kathy that she had met a man who was very wealthy and liked to travel. She talked about moving to work on this man's ranch, which Kathy thought was in Oklahoma. While she didn't know how Sheila had met this man, she told Brown her sister was "big on using the Internet."

Kathy also acknowledged to Brown that sometime ago she had found some BDSM-related literature at Sheila's residence. Based on this literature, she said, she believed Sheila was involved in BDSM and had a spanking fetish. However, she added, they had never spoken directly about the taboo subject. She also said that she and her other sister, Michelle Fox, had each received a letter from Sheila around Christmas 1995. Both were typewritten, postmarked in the Netherlands and bore Sheila and Debbie's signatures at the bottom.

Brown didn't waste any time. The next morning, the task force put out a press release asking for the public's assistance in locating the Faiths. Anyone who knew the mother and daughter were asked to call a toll-free number with information. "According to family members, Sheila and Debbie are believed to have left Fullerton, California, in 1994 to move to Colorado," the press release stated. "After spending a few months in Colorado, they again moved to the Kansas/Oklahoma area. Family members have not had contact with them since. Debbie Faith has been restricted to a wheelchair since birth. Sheila and Debbie have known connections with John Robinson."

That same day, about sixty people packed the courtroom for Robinson's first court appearance since his arrest. The defendant, now represented by the Kansas Death Penalty Defense Unit, was not required to enter a plea. His new attorneys—Ron Evans, Christian Zoller and Mark Manna—received a copy of

to Colorado. Sheila, very lonely after her husband's death in 1991, had followed her friend to Colorado in 1993.

Nancy Guerrero said that Sheila was very vulnerable and attempted to meet men through personal ads and the Internet. She said that around 1994 Sheila mentioned meeting a "well-to-do" man named John. He had promised to take care of them financially. "He told her he was going to take her on a cruise, that he would take care of her daughter, that she'd never have to work, that money was no problem," Guerrero said. "He promised her the world."

In June or July of that year, Sheila told Nancy she was going to visit her parents for a couple of weeks and asked her friend if she could pick up her mail. Nancy had been with them the night before they left, helping them pack for the trip, and said Sheila had talked only about visiting her family in Texas. When she went back the next day at 9:30 A.M., they were gone. Sheila drove a white 1978 Chevy Van, Nancy said, with a lift in the middle to load Debbie up in her wheelchair.

Guerrero told Lininger that she became suspicious when she went to the Faiths' home and there was no mail in the box. She went to the post office and learned that her mail had been forwarded to a post office box in Olathe, Kansas. Nancy's daughter, Melissa, also said that Debbie had mentioned they were possibly going to stop in Kansas on the way. When she called Sheila's family, she learned that they never showed up in Texas. About a month later, Guerrero called the Olathe Police Department and reported what she knew, but she never heard back. She never heard from Sheila and Debbie, either, which was highly unusual because of their close friendship.

On Monday, June 19, the investigation was scaled back to twelve detectives from Lenexa, Overland Park and Raymore. Boyer had returned to work, Brown had been relieved of his press duties and Wilson was still on board. Reed and Roth brought them—as well as Hohnholt, Batt and Beyer—into the police department's library and told them what they knew about Tiffany. "A tight lid was still on the news," Roth said.

son as her uncle. "I refused to comment," Roth said. "But the cat was coming out of the bag!"

The story hit the newspaper the following Tuesday, June 27. CHILD MISSING SINCE 1985 MAY BE ALIVE, trumpeted *The Kansas City Star*. Scott Canon reported that police were investigating whether Tiffany was living under another name in the suburbs of a Midwestern state. Contacting the household, the *Star* had been told "no comment" by a woman who had come to the door. A lawyer who had been retained by the family would say only that they were "cooperating fully with law enforcement."

The paper noted that the case presented legal and ethical issues because the 15-year-old girl, who had recently finished her freshman year in high school, was still a minor. It also quoted sources knowledgeable about the investigation as saying that she could have been raised by a couple that Robinson knew without ever being legally adopted.

Only the day before, Roth had received the FedExed footprints of Don and Frieda's daughter from the FBI and dispatched Wilson to Truman Medical to pick up Tiffany's records. They sent both sets of prints to the lab for comparison. At 7:00 P.M., June 29, Roth was at home when he received a page from Wilson. "Bingo, it's Tiffany," Roth wrote in his journal that night.

On July 5, Morrison called a meeting at the DA's office to discuss what they had on the old cases. Reed and Wilson were there from Overland Park; Meier and Roth came from Lenexa; Gary Dirks and Keith Kerr from the Johnson County Crime Lab; Brunell from the FBI and Frank Booth from the Kansas City, Missouri, Crime Lab. Kerr had bad news. They had all hoped there would be a match on the typing from Tiffany Stasi's doctored adoption papers with those on the letters in the Clampitt and Godfrey cases. But it wasn't to be. There was no match. The group then asked Kerr to examine letters that several of the women (including Trouten, Bonner and the Faiths) had purportedly written to their loved ones

Two weeks after graduating from eighth grade in June 1993, however, Debbie and her mother picked up and moved to Santa Cruz, California. Her mom had met somebody, Suzanne said. The last day before she left, Debbie broke into tears as she gave Suzanne a crystal necklace. "It's beautiful," Suzanne said, her voice cracking with emotion ten years later. "She was always wearing it around her neck. She said, 'This is a reason for me to come back to you.' I still keep it in a black suede bag in my jewelry box at my mom's house."

Debbie and Sheila didn't stay in Santa Cruz for long, Suzanne said. The relationship with the man didn't work out and they decided to follow their friends the Guerreros, who had moved to Pueblo, Colorado. Suzanne kept in constant touch with Debbie by telephone, however, running up monstrous telephone bills as they chatted about everything under the sun.

By the summer of 1994, Debbie told Suzanne that her mother had met a new man. "She said she was going to drive out to Kansas City to meet up with a guy named John that her mom had met through the Internet or newspaper," Suzanne said. "She said he had a farm and she was finally going to be able to ride horses. This guy made her mom happy and she couldn't wait to meet him."

But Suzanne instantly had a bad feeling about the trip. "I can sense when something is wrong," she said. "I had a feeling that she should not go there and I said, 'Try to talk your mom out of it.' But she said, 'Oh no, it's fine. He seems like a very nice guy. My mom is happy.' She said, 'I'm leaving tonight and I'll call you tomorrow as soon as I get there.' But no call ever came."

Though she didn't want to believe it, Suzanne was certain her friend was gone long before she saw pictures of Debbie and Sheila plastered on the news in June 2000. "I started getting worried the next day when she didn't call," she said. When others tried to comfort her by saying Debbie was probably just having too much fun to call, Suzanne knew otherwise. "I said,

He also came across a message fragment from Robinson to the Michigan woman, demanding her usernames and passwords, and Suzette's reply, providing all she had.

Because Robinson reportedly had been using the online handle, "The Slavemaster" and the name had garnered such widespread media attention, Jacobson felt obligated to check it out. He ran a "Grep string search" on the computers using EnCase from Guidance Software. "A grep string search includes all of the known files, contents of deleted files and any other area on the hard drive," Jacobson said. "If 'Slavemaster' was used recently by JR, grep probably would have found it. Not to mention the lack of any plain view communications to him or from him, using that name. In all the months I worked on those computers, I never once found any evidence he used that handle."

The origination of the erroneous "Slavemaster" handle would remain a mystery. "I'd like to know myself where the name came from," Jacobson said. "I'm almost certain it's a result of people calling in to the media saying they'd talked to someone online who called himself 'The Slavemaster'— thinking it was JR. It's a great name, but he never used it. Factoid: If JR did use 'Slavemaster,' in the BDSM world, that would be about as original as calling yourself 'Smith.' JR liked to think he was rather clever."

On the contrary, Jacobson said he was not convinced that Robinson was all that savvy about computer technology. "JR is a liar and a con man," he said. "The computer was just another tool to that end and he used it well in the context of a con. He was not good enough to cover his tracks, nor did he really understand how the Internet works. Ultimately, that was his fatal mistake. I would say his computer knowledge was approximately a seventh grade level of expertise."

Of all the incriminating material recovered by Jacobson and Hill, however, arguably the most intriguing find was the pager software discovered on a floppy disk near Robinson's desktop. "I found 30+ pages of pager messages to a person I

difference, your parents, etc. I will be receiving a copy of the article by e-mail later and will forward it to you."

Robinson demonstrated effusive affection toward his girl-friend on many occasions. "Happy Birthday to you, Happy Birthday to you! You're 20 years old and I love you," he gushed on April 11, 1998. At other times, however, he expressed frustration or anger when she apparently exercised some independence. "It really pisses me off when I have to hunt for you," he lectured her a few months later. "I have beeped you five fucking times and told you to call. My anger is building by the moment! I am tired and do not have patience for this shit!"

In the middle of all these messages, Robinson would receive a reality check in the form of pages from his wife Nancy, telling him to come home or to fix something around Santa Barbara Estates. One time, she said the county had called and was offering him a job as a meter reader. Detectives were left shaking their heads at the absurdity of it all.

The pager messages, however, helped to resolve one mystery: the blank stationery in Robinson's office containing fake letterheads from the CIA, White House, Drug Enforcement Administration, Department of Justice and State Department. "After reviewing the 'pages,'" Roth said, "we had no doubt that Lewicka had been the proud recipient of several letters from the leaders of government extolling the virtues of John Robinson."

Brad Hill also made some key discoveries in his analysis of Suzette's computer. First of all, he investigated the Web site that Suzette was supposedly developing for Robinson about a secret BDSM society called the International Council of Masters. "Like everything else in JR's life, it was a figment of his overactive imagination," Hill said. "Although there were several references in Suzette's computer, my opinion is that he had her build this Web site to keep her busy while he got her ready to go on her 'trip.'"

Hill also created a profile of Suzette's computer in the final hours of her life. He was able to see that she had spent some

with parental custody in brokering the phony adoption of her infant daughter, Tiffany. Morrison told reporters that the child was now living with a Midwestern couple who had illegally adopted her fifteen years earlier.

The couple knew Robinson before they adopted the girl, he said, and gave him money that they thought was to cover legitimate adoption fees. He added that investigators did not believe the couple, whom he refused to name, had any knowledge that the adoption was not legal. "There is paperwork that would appear to be genuine if you didn't know any better," the prosecutor said.

Morrison said that Tiffany was now a teenager, aware of the investigation and struggling to come to terms with the situation. He said he wanted to try and limit her involvement in the case and that his office might help to arrange a meeting between the girl and her blood relatives, who maintained that they had no intention of seeking custody. "I think everybody wants what is best for this kid," he stated.

The prosecutor also said that detectives in Overland Park and Lenexa were continuing to investigate the disappearances of Catherine Clampitt and Paula Godfrey. While they had also investigated Lisa and Tiffany's disappearances in the 1980s, Overland Park police chief John Douglass said, "It wouldn't have been possible to prosecute then, with much less evidence."

Tiffany's family—still unnamed—released a statement through Agent Tarpley, who read it aloud after Morrison had announced the new charges: "We love our daughter very much. Since her adoption, which was never kept from her, we have always assumed that as she became an adult, she would be curious about her birth family. Because we were unaware whom her birth family was, it was our intention to assist her in any way possible in her efforts in identifying and locating them."

The couple, through Tarpley, also appealed for the media's continued cooperation in protecting the girl from publicity: "The circumstances surrounding the investigation of John Robinson are as distressing to our immediate family as they

for his reaction to the news. Under a tentative agreement brokered by Morrison, he had only recently consented to a blood test which proved that he was Tiffany's father. In return, her adoptive parents had said they would allow him to get in touch with her for a possible meeting. "I'm just upset, okay? . . . You can't even imagine how I feel," Stasi reportedly said.

And Karen Moore, Lisa Stasi's aunt, appealed to the media to respect the child's privacy. "She's fifteen years old," she said. "She's got to be having a really tough time with this. School is getting ready to start and it's got to be very hard for her. I'm hoping everyone will be just as delicate with her now as they have been for the past couple of months."

Over the fall, Lisa and Carl's relatives attempted several times to contact Heather Robinson. Tiffany's biological father wrote to the girl on her sixteenth birthday. His sister, Kathy Klinginsmith, also wrote several times, sending gifts and a flower basket for Halloween. But there had been no reply. "The only thing I can assume is that they are trying to stall and delay all they can," Seth Shumaker, Carl Stasi's attorney in Kirksville, Missouri, told *The Kansas City Star*. "It's frustrating. You believe people are telling you the truth and dealing with you in a gentlemanly manner, and then their promises don't hold up. It pushes you to an adversarial position."

Her maternal grandmother, Pat Sylvester, had better luck. She had received a card from the family but refused to disclose whether it was from Heather or her parents and what it had said. She noted that she was just trying to be patient and hoped one day to meet her granddaughter.

Stasi's adoption and one count each of aggravated sexual battery and felony theft involving his encounter with Neufeld. The judge sided with defense attorneys in only one instance, dismissing the aggravated sexual battery charge involving Milliron whose testimony at the preliminary hearing did not convince the court that her sadomasochistic encounter with Robinson was nonconsensual.

Defense attorneys had maintained in legal filings that the evidence was insufficient to show that any crimes occurred in Johnson County. But Anderson agreed with prosecutors that virtually all of the evidence showed Robinson's involvement with the women was in Johnson County and that Linn County was nothing more than a dumping ground for bodies. "The court is convinced that the venue is proper," he said.

Anderson entered pleas of not guilty on Robinson's behalf after defense attorney Ron Evans said his client would "stand silent" to the charges. Morrison then handed Robinson's attorneys written notice that he would seek the death penalty if Robinson was to be convicted. The defendant only spoke once at the Friday-morning hearing. When asked by the judge whether he agreed to waive his right to a speedy trial within ninety days, Robinson said, "That's right, Your Honor."

The judge's ruling coincided with an event of momentous significance to those involved. ADA Sara Welch had been prosecuting an aggravated robbery case out of Lenexa and one of Roth's detectives was scheduled to testify. However, he had a family event he wanted to attend that, as luck would have it, was right in the middle of her trial. The detective had gone to Roth to solicit his help in the matter. Roth called Welch, and after complaining a little bit, she said she'd do what she could.

"I went out of my way to get one of Rick's detectives on and off the stand so he could attend some music function at which his daughter was performing," Welch remembered. "It was a hassle, but I did it. I was none too gracious about it. You have to understand that when I am in a jury trial, nothing else matters.

tain grounds for an appeal, Paul Morrison insisted that Thomas be provided some assistance. Even though Thomas was a "fine young attorney," Morrison said he was taking on an assignment that would be overwhelming for any single lawyer—even one who had substantial experience with capital cases. Thomas had only a few jury trials under his belt and never had defended anyone facing the death penalty. "I don't want to try this case twice and I know he doesn't, either," Morrison argued.

Judge Anderson called the situation a head-on clash between the two parts of the Sixth Amendment. Robinson had the right to hire any lawyer he wanted, the judge explained. But he also had the right to be represented by a lawyer with the necessary qualifications for a complex capital murder case. He asked Evans whether he or other lawyers from his office would be willing to remain on the case as co-counsel to Thomas, who had insisted on being the lead attorney. Evans, however, repeated his earlier stance that it was not a "workable situation," since Robinson had hired his own attorney, which made him ineligible for representation from the state-financed office. "I don't see any statutory mechanism that allows you to keep us," Evans told the judge.

After meeting privately with Robinson and his new attorney a few days later, Judge Anderson said he had determined that the defendant was "partly indigent"—in that there was no way he could afford to pay for effective representation—and therefore qualified to receive appointed legal assistance. He allowed the Kansas Death Penalty Defense Unit to withdraw from the case. The fact that Robinson could have kept the unit's services for free but chose to hire a private lawyer "speaks for the relationship between Mr. Robinson and our office," Evans told the judge.

Because Kansas had only reinstated the death penalty in 1994, only a few lawyers in the state had even handled capital cases. So it wasn't terribly surprising that Judge Anderson appointed on August 1 two Missouri attorneys, Sean O'Brien and Patrick Berrigan, to assist Thomas in the complex case.

his previous clients who had been in jail with Robinson could be called as a witness because he was claiming that the defendant told him crime details no one else knew.

Thomas was referring to a convicted thief named Marvin Ray. In a letter to prosecutors in the summer of 2001, Ray apparently had offered to testify about his conversations with Robinson while the two were incarcerated at the Johnson County Jail. However, a subsequent search of Ray's cell turned up a three-page handwritten letter in which Ray allegedly admitted he had helped a woman and a man—not Robinson—take the bodies of two women from Topeka to a farm in Linn County, Kansas, in exchange for two pounds of crack cocaine.

In the February 21 hearing, Thomas complained that prosecutors had turned the letter over to him only the week before, and he said he felt he could not continue to represent Robinson and maintain his ethical obligation to his former client. Based on his withdrawal request, Berrigan and O'Brien, the two defense lawyers who had been appointed to help Thomas, asked the judge to postpone the trial by yet another four months because they would have to shoulder Thomas's workload.

However, Morrison said the state had no intention of calling Ray as a witness. Robinson had made veiled allegations that others had information about the women's deaths, but authorities didn't believe him. "We absolutely believe Mr. Robinson manufactured that evidence," Morrison said of the letter found in Ray's jail cell. When Morrison said he wanted to file written objections to the motions, the judge agreed to take up the matter on Thursday, February 28, 2002.

The following week, after reading Morrison's objections, Judge Anderson agreed to dismiss Thomas from the defense team, but only after Robinson had agreed.

"Do you, then, discharge Mr. Thomas as your attorney?" the judge asked the defendant.

After conferring with Thomas, Robinson replied, "Yes, sir, Your Honor."

among law enforcement that Robinson had disposed of bodies in a location that had been excavated and covered over by concrete. "They didn't make any admissions, but I think they were all talking about theories."

In the discussion that the prosecutors held with the defense, it was not clear that Robinson had admitted any crimes even to his own lawyers, who steadfastly refused to comment on the case. But as Morrison knew, top-notch lawyers like Berrigan and O'Brien were adept at establishing a relationship with clients in which they could talk hypothetically. "It might very well be that he hadn't per se admitted anything to them," Morrison said. "But they had to at least have said, 'Hey, without you admitting anything to us right now, do we have permission to lay a hypothetical scenario out to prosecutors?'"

It was a moot point, in any case. Morrison and Welch were not interested in cutting any deals with Robinson. They held several discussions about how they would like to bring closure for the families of the three women and even discussed it with Bill Godfrey and other family members. "Frankly, I think they were surprised we didn't take [the offer]," Morrison said. "I felt pretty good about saying no. It was repugnant that someone like John Robinson thought he could continue to use [these women] as if they were bargaining chips."

Morrison also said that Robinson had been lying his entire life and he didn't believe for a minute that he was suddenly going to turn over a new leaf. Even if he actually told them what he'd done and where the bodies were located, "how would you know what to believe?" Morrison asked. "He's a guy who would take great joy in misleading us and feeding a line of BS to these families and laughing about it inside. He had no credibility with us."

By the end of August, Robinson's court-appointed attorneys had grown even more insistent, asking the judge the next month to delay the trial or else remove them from the case. They accused Anderson of being insensitive and unresponsive to their pleas for more time and said they could not and

In another move that upset the media, Anderson also ruled that jury selection would be closed to the public. He argued that potential jurors should feel free to answer personal questions candidly and said he was concerned they might be influenced by the presence of the media. In response to his ruling, however, several local outlets voiced their displeasure and quickly filed an appeal to the Kansas Supreme Court.

On September 11, as part of their progressively preposterous pretrial motions, Robinson's lawyers asked the judge to dismiss the entire panel of twelve hundred prospective Johnson County jurors that were supposed to begin reporting to the courthouse in five days.

Earlier in the year, the defense had presented a survey showing that 94 percent of the county's residents knew of the case and 67 percent of those thought Robinson was "definitely" or "probably" guilty. In the last-minute motion, the defense said questionnaires filled out by the prospective jurors only reinforced the earlier survey results. "They demonstrate widespread awareness of the case, extensive factual recall . . . and widespread opinions about Mr. Robinson's guilt . . . and the appropriate sentence," the defense argued.

While he ignored the defense request to throw out the panel, Judge Anderson granted them permission the next day to send Robinson for medical testing at the University of Kansas Medical Center, as long as it did not interfere with regular courtroom proceedings. In asking for the medical examination, the defense said that New York psychiatrist Dorothy Lewis had talked to Robinson and members of his family and suspected that he suffered from a bipolar mood disorder. "History obtained independently of Mr. Robinson reflects that as many as four generations of family members may have suffered from such psychiatric illness similar to his," the defense wrote in a brief.

Lewis, a professor of psychiatry at New York University School of Medicine, was quoted by the defense as saying that Robinson also "has a history of severe physical and emotional

Chapter 23

It was a crisp, clear Monday in mid-September when the first of twelve hundred potential jurors—the largest number the county had ever called in a single case—began reporting for duty at the redbrick courthouse in downtown Olathe. Court officials handed each potential juror a tag with a number and instructions not to discuss the proceedings with anyone. Shuffling them in large groups upstairs to a windowless fourth-floor courtroom, they began the painstaking process of selecting the twelve jurors and five alternates who would ultimately decide Robinson's fate.

Judge John Anderson III welcomed each group to his wood-paneled courtroom and introduced them to the cast of characters who would occupy center stage throughout the high-profile trial, including prosecutors Morrison and Welch and Robinson's defense team—Pat Berrigan, Sean O'Brien, Joseph Luby and Jason Billam. Even the fifty-eight-year-old defendant, looking thin and pale but sharply dressed in a suit and tie, stood and bowed slightly, offering a brief smile and a pleasant "good morning." Security was tight, with as many as six uniformed deputies standing guard outside the door.

Anderson began proceedings much like a teacher on the first day of school—asking jurors with hardship requests to stand or raise their hands. Those who did were brought back in small groups of six, starting that afternoon, to explain why they should be excused. Most of the requests came from those who said they would suffer financially because they were self-employed or had employers who would not pay

Robinson from watching the nightly news or reading *The Kansas City Star.* A large number who were subsequently dismissed had already made up their minds. "He's guilty as charged," insisted a woman, No. 17. "I can't imagine anything that would change my mind," agreed a man, No. 328. "He's guilty. He's sick. He's playing the court," said No. 357. "I might not be the most impartial juror, but at this point, who could be?" asked No. 327.

Berrigan took to using a chart he had devised to illustrate the two phases of a capital murder case. The state, he explained, was alleging that Robinson had committed two counts of capital murder by killing Suzette Trouten and Izabela Lewicka and one count of first-degree murder in the death of Lisa Stasi. For a defendant to be found guilty of capital murder, he went on, the state must prove beyond a reasonable doubt that the crimes were intentional, premeditated and met one of seven special circumstances outlined by Kansas law. In Robinson's case, the state was alleging the special circumstance was that the murders were "part of a common scheme or plan" involving the six women in Kansas and Missouri.

Only if Robinson was unanimously convicted of capital murder would the jury enter the penalty phase, where they would be required to consider aggravating and mitigating factors. Under Kansas law, there was a list of eight possible aggravating factors and nine possible mitigating factors. There was also a broader category of mitigating factors that the defense could choose to present. "They could include, for example, any evidence about a person's background and how they were raised, or if they were subjected to a horrific abusive childhood," said Berrigan, who was believed to be hinting at defense strategy. "The Supreme Court has also recognized mercy as a mitigating circumstance."

Mitigating factors would not have to be proven beyond a reasonable doubt, Berrigan said, and the jury would not assess them as a group. They would consider them individually

weeks than I ever have before," said one man, No. 14, who hadn't made up his mind. Another man said he believed in capital punishment in theory but was "not very comfortable" with the idea of actually sentencing someone to death. "I never thought I would be a part of it," said No. 5. "It would be something that I'd think about every day until the day I die." One woman, No. 244, actually thought death was too easy. "Life," she said, "would be a harsher penalty."

No. 152 was easily the most radical proponent. He said he firmly believed that Robinson was guilty and should die for his crimes, but he also thought capital punishment in the United States was too benign. He recalled a case in Pakistan where an accused serial murderer of children was convicted and executed by hanging. Afterward, his body was chopped into a hundred pieces in front of young witnesses, he said. After suggesting that Robinson deserved the same treatment, he was excused.

Court officials had originally estimated that jury selection would take only a week. Within the first few days, however, Anderson had delayed the start of testimony to Monday, September 30, noting that the court would need more time for the thorough questioning necessary to selecting jurors in a capital murder case. "We have never been through a process of this magnitude," he said. At the end of the second week, Anderson again delayed testimony—this time to Monday, October 7. In a sign that they were approaching the finish line, however, he announced that the court would not need to summons the remaining six hundred potential jurors who had been on standby.

By Wednesday, October 2, after approving 83 of the more than 250 potential jurors they had interviewed, the court was ready to begin the third phase of the selection process. Calling in the first forty, Anderson explained that the attorneys would now be asking another round of questions. They would do the same with the forty-three remaining jurors the next day, he said, and then pick the panel at 1:30 P.M. on Friday. For

fense. He also worried aloud that too much of the earlier questioning had centered on the death penalty and not enough on presumption of innocence. "For the last two and a half weeks, we've spent a lot of time talking about punishment and it's sort of like putting the cart before the horse," he said. "I'm concerned that some of you might think that's all this case is about. Are there any people here who think Robinson is guilty [but haven't spoken up] because we've spent all this time talking about the death penalty?"

After several hours of questioning, the court eliminated just seven of the forty prospective jurors. They included a Secret Service agent who knew several detectives who worked the case, a woman who was squeamish at the thought of gory pictures, another woman who said she would hold it against Robinson if he didn't testify and a man who had trouble with Robinson's sadomasochistic practices. The court also dismissed a woman who listed Morrison as one of her personal heroes, right along with George Bush and Oprah Winfrey. "Your Honor, I think he came after Oprah," O'Brien joked, proving that he might be defending a serial killer, but he still had a sense of humor. Even Robinson smiled.

The next day brought an interesting story, latched onto by media hungry for a human interest angle. When Berrigan asked if any of the forty-three prospective jurors knew each other, No. 316 stood and said he knew No. 454. "And how do you know Miss 454?" asked Berrigan. "She's been my spouse for thirty-eight years," No. 316 answered. There were peals of laughter in the courtroom and those present marveled at the odds of two married jurors surviving several rounds of the winnowing process.

Berrigan chuckled, too, but in the end he protested the ability of the couple to be independent thinkers and told the judge he was particularly worried they wouldn't be able to weigh aggravating and mitigating factors individually. "Mr. Robinson is entitled to twelve people making their own decisions," he said. "We don't need to put them to the test."

twelve strikes each to arrive at the finalists. There was complete silence as Morrison and Berrigan took turns jotting down their strikes on white pieces of paper, handing their ballots to bailiff Pam Langenfeld, who solemnly carried them to Anderson and to court reporter Annette Pascarelli.

When they were done, Anderson read off the numbers one at a time. As he did so, those who had been called left their seats in the gallery and stepped to the bench to make sure their numbers matched the names on the judge's list. Within fifteen minutes, seven women and five men of varying ages had taken their seats in the jury box. Calling upon fifteen more finalists, the court repeated the process to select four men and a woman as alternates. The married couple, however, didn't make the final cut. The husband had been struck as an alternate; his wife was among fifteen not even considered. Most who were dismissed showed little emotion, but at least one woman broke into tears of joy as she left the courtroom.

While the seventeen-member panel remained seated in the jury box, Anderson stressed the importance of court orders that prohibited them from talking about the case or letting anyone discuss it in their presence. Though they would not be sequestered, he said, they would be closely supervised. Instead of coming to the courthouse individually each morning, they would meet at a central location and take a bus. They would be kept together for lunch and bused back to their cars in the evening. To ensure anonymity, they would continue to be known only by their numbers. Issuing his "simple but very important" admonishments, the judge released his new charges until Monday morning.

"This investigation culminated in the execution of many search warrants," Morrison carefully explained to the court. "Discovered were many, many personal items belonging to each woman found at the Olathe storage locker rented by the defendant as well as the Linn County farm. A lot of what these women owned were jewelry, Social Security cards, identification documents, high school diplomas, birth certificates.

"Also found at the Olathe storage locker was a briefcase," he continued. "There were stacks of preaddressed letters and cards to relatives of Suzette Trouten ready to be mailed for birthdays and whatnot. The investigation uncovered that those alimony checks that Dr. Bonner was sending to his [ex-] wife, Beverly, they went into the defendant's account. Those Social Security checks [for Sheila and Debbie Faith] that kept coming for years to that P.O. Box in Olathe, they, too, were cashed by the defendant and went into his bank accounts. Evidence will show . . . that the defendant went to elaborate means to have all these letters sent from all over to make it appear as though these ladies were still alive. The evidence will show that when Tiffany Stasi disappeared, in fact, a baby was given to the defendant's brother to raise as their own by the defendant.

"During the course of this case we'll expose many elaborate scams by the defendant. Scams to steal their money, scams to exploit them sexually, scams to kill them, scams to cover up their deaths." By the time the state finished constructing the last days of each of the women's lives, Morrison concluded, "the evidence will be crystal clear that the defendant has been killing women for over 17 years."

But one of Robinson's four attorneys insisted that, although his client may have known or been sexually involved with the women, he didn't kill them. He also stressed that the defense had come into the case late and was unprepared for trial—an argument they would make several times in the next several weeks. "This is a very humbling experience because . . . we don't know what we need to know to effectively defend our client," said defense lawyer Sean O'Brien. In fact,

physically abused as children or had unusually cold parents. You're going to hear a lot of evidence about this culture. We're not saying that [Lewicka and Trouten] deserved anything bad to happen to them because they were involved in BDSM—it's just an important aspect of this case. We will try to handle this subject as sensitively and tastefully as we can."

In order to convict Robinson of capital murder, O'Brien argued that the state had to prove he murdered all six women as part of a common scheme or plan. Yet the circumstances surrounding their deaths were so different from one another and occurred so far apart in time, he said, that prosecutors could not possibly prevail.

"The evidence in this case isn't there," O'Brien told the jury. "Not just because of the questions we have surrounding the case but because of the circumstances of each of these women and their relationship to John, if any, is completely different and they span more than 15 years. We don't know anything that indicates the disappearance of Lisa Stasi in 1985 had anything to do with Izabela Lewicka or Suzette Trouten. This is important because if you don't find beyond a reasonable doubt that there's a common scheme or course of conduct, then you have to acquit Mr. Robinson of capital murder."

O'Brien spoke in a rambling manner about each of Robinson's alleged victims. "Lisa [Stasi] and [her husband] Carl, you'll find, had a relationship that was very turbulent," he said. "They had problems with drugs and alcohol abuse and addiction. They fought frequently and often those fights were physical. And to make matters worse, they lived with Carl's family who strongly disapproved of Lisa living there. They didn't like her. In late December Carl told Lisa the marriage was over and that he was re-enlisting in the Navy. He left Lisa alone with the baby and didn't make any provisions for their care. Carl's family thought Lisa partied too much. When Carl left town, they pretty much rejected her and she ended up in a battered women's shelter temporarily. She would stop by

that to be true," O'Brien asserted. "It may or may not be. We don't really know why Beverly Bonner was killed. We do know that at least one person other than John Robinson gained financially from Beverly Bonner's death."

(Several sources familiar with the case later said they believed O'Brien was referring to a man who was an acquaintance of Robinson's and whose name had appeared in his red address book. Interviewed by police not long after Robinson's June 2000 arrest, this individual reported that he had met the defendant in the early 1990s but didn't know him well. He said Robinson approached him in 1994, saying that his "aunt," whom he did not name, had fallen in love and was planning to move overseas. She was apparently tired of storing her personal property in a storage facility and had asked Robinson to get rid of it. Robinson asked this individual to help him remove the items from a storage locker in Raymore, Missouri, presumably Stor-Mor For Less, and to hold a garage sale, which he did at the home of a friend. Over the course of about two weeks, Robinson's acquaintance said he sold many of the items— couches, beds, dressers and a lot of women's clothing—and netted about $2,000. Robinson allowed him to keep 25 percent of the proceeds but took the rest for himself, he said.)

O'Brien moved on to the Faiths. "Debbie and Sheila Faith came to Kansas City in 1994 with a van that was outfitted for Debbie, who was in a wheelchair," he stated. "We know the van they drove was sold, but not by John Robinson. We know that the electric lift in the van that was to accommodate Debbie's wheelchair was also sold, but not by John Robinson. We know the wheelchair was sold, but not by John Robinson. The person who sold them was interviewed twice by police and apparently withheld that information. This was the same person who moved Beverly Bonner's belongings into that storage facility. Other items belonging to the Faiths ended up in a garage sale in the south part of Kansas City. That garage sale was being held by a man who says he has never met John Robinson."

parents about why she was coming to Kansas City. She told them she was coming here to the Art Institute and in reality she was coming here for a BDSM relationship. . . . We also know that John Robinson paid her rent and gave her money to live on. . . . She also enrolled in classes in the Junior College. She took lessons in martial arts and fencing and art classes and John Robinson paid for those courses. . . . It's also true that she worked on a magazine that was produced and published by John Robinson called *Manufactured Modular Home Living*. It's a magazine that's . . . directed specifically to people who live in mobile home communities. John did business through a bank account for the publication, which he called Specialty Publications, and many of Izabela's activities were funded through that account. In fact, she did design some of the artwork on the covers of various issues and helped to lay out the magazine. So . . . in addition to their personal and sexual relationship, there was also that business relationship. . . . Although her first contact with John Robinson was over the Internet for bondage and discipline purposes, their relationship became much, much more serious . . . John Robinson's relationship with Izabela Lewicka lasted over two years."

The disappearance of Suzette Trouten caused police to focus on John Robinson, O'Brien said. But the prosecution's charge that Suzette had been lured to Kansas under false pretenses was inaccurate. "John met her through an ad that she herself placed on the Internet," O'Brien stated. "She placed the ad and John responded to it. It was not an ad for a job. She was not looking for employment. It was an ad for a dominant bondage and discipline partner. . . . She was obviously a troubled young woman. She had a self-inflicted gunshot wound in the abdomen. . . . She appeared to have a good relationship with her mother and the rest of her family. But . . . she frequently and regularly deceived her mother about where she was going and what she was doing and who she was with and why she was going there because she didn't want her mother to know that she was involved in the BDSM lifestyle. She told

Chapter 25

Suzette's mother was the first witness for the prosecution to take the stand on the sunny afternoon of October 7, describing the close relationship she had shared with her youngest daughter, a nurse's aide who dreamed of completing her education. Wearing a pale flowery pantsuit with a pink blouse, the petite blond-haired woman nervously clasped and unclasped her hands as she testified before a crowded courtroom. "We talked on the phone almost every day," Carolyn stated. "I thought we talked about everything."

But Trouten told Morrison that she didn't know her daughter was involved in the BDSM lifestyle. "Would you have approved?" Morrison asked. "Oh no!" she replied. She said her daughter had told her about meeting a man on the Internet named John Robinson, but he was a wealthy businessman with international connections, who purportedly offered a $65,000 salary if Suzette would move to Kansas and care for his elderly father. The job would entail a lot of travel, Carolyn said.

After taking two trips to Kansas City in the fall of 1999, she said Suzette decided to take Robinson up on his offer, packing up her belongings and driving out in mid-February 2000. For a few weeks, she stayed in close touch via e-mail and telephone. At 1:00 A.M. (EST) on March 1, she called for the last time, her mother said. "I said, 'What are you doing up at this hour?'" testified Carolyn, who added that she was getting ready to close the restaurant for the night. "She said she wasn't tired and she wanted to let me know they'd be leaving

He added, "Any master . . . doesn't want the slave to fucking be touched by anyone else."

The Canadian woman was heard steering the subject toward Trouten's disappearance. "I haven't heard squat from anyone as far as Suzette is concerned," she told him. "I've got a PI (private investigator) working on it," he replied. "From what he tells me, she went to Mexico and is sailing around. All he can do is trace the credit cards and gas receipts. . . . I just wish she'd do the right thing and get ahold of people and let them know what's going on."

Remington testified that she had forwarded any and all information she received from Robinson to the Lenexa Police Department, which had launched a full-scale investigation into Robinson.

"Were you playing him?" Welch asked Remington.

"Yes," she said. "If I was cold and aloof, he would have stopped all communication."

As 5:00 P.M. approached on the first day of testimony, Judge Anderson dismissed the jury. The court, however, wasn't done with Remington and he asked if she could be counted on to show up the next day.

"No," she answered firmly, to the surprise of many sitting in the courtroom.

Upon hearing her response, the judge slapped her with a $25,000 material-witness bond and placed her under arrest. She would be spending the night in the Johnson County Jail.

Remington returned to the stand the next morning, October 8, wearing a plaid flannel shirt, faded blue jeans and a defiant demeanor. Before the jury was called in, defense attorneys argued that some of the e-mails she had received were tainted because of questions about the time they had been sent. After listening to Remington's explanation, however, the judge disagreed. "Technology creates evidentiary problems quicker than we can create solutions," he said, ruling to admit the e-mails into evidence.

The reluctant witness admitted to the court that she had

and Trouten's after meeting them in a BDSM chat room a few years earlier. Taylor added that she had met Trouten several times in Michigan and engaged in sadomasochistic sex with her on one occasion. Shortly after her friend disappeared, Remington told her she was communicating with a master who somehow knew Trouten, she said. "I thought it sounded suspicious," Taylor testified. "I said, 'Ask the gentleman if he knows another gentleman who would be interested in me.'"

A short time later, Remington e-mailed Taylor with the name and address of another man named Tom. Taylor wrote to him and soon heard back. "He was seeking a full-time slave," she said, noting in one e-mail that he wanted her to move to Kansas City. "He wanted somebody to serve his every whim." At one point, Taylor said she asked Tom for a reference. "I wanted to confirm that he was a genuine master and basically a nice guy," she said. Tom put her in communication with someone she knew only as Slavedancer, who vouched for him via e-mail.

Taylor said Tom also called her and left two voice mail messages. Morrison played one of the messages left on her machine, giving her a new e-mail address and checking on her well-being. The voice heard on the machine said he was "getting anxious" about meeting Taylor and wanted to hear from her soon. "I worry and I don't like to be kept in the dark," he said, sounding identical to the man who called himself JT and had been heard talking the day before to Remington.

All the while, Taylor and Remington were conferring with one another about Tom and JT. "We felt that the same man that was e-mailing me was e-mailing her," Taylor said. Both women were forwarding their correspondence to Detective Jake Boyer of the Lenexa Police Department, they said. Like Remington, Taylor said she only continued to stay in touch with Tom in order to find out more about Trouten. "I wanted to build his trust," she said. "I wanted to find out about Suzette."

"Did the e-mails continue?" asked prosecutor Paul Morrison.

"Until John Robinson was arrested," Taylor replied.

ballistic," she testified. "He was cursing up one side and down the other. It kind of shook me up. He got so upset so fast."

Glines said that three pastel-colored letters ultimately came a few days later and were addressed to either Minnesota or Michigan. She also remembered that there was no return address but only the name Suzette or the initials ST.

Shortly after she mailed the letters on March 27, 2000, her relationship with Robinson ended, she said.

Marshella Chidester, Suzette's aunt and godmother, followed Glines to the stand and identified several of her niece's personal belongings, including a desk lamp and a yellow legal pad containing the names, birthdays and addresses of various family members. She also identified cards and letters signed by Suzette that the family received after her disappearance, including the letters that Glines had just testified about mailing for Robinson from California. "We hadn't heard from her over the telephone for a couple of weeks," she said sadly, "I couldn't understand why she hadn't called."

Contents of the letters piqued their suspicions even further, Marshella said, including odd references in a typewritten letter sent from Mexico to her and her husband shortly before Suzette's body was discovered. Chidester confirmed that the signature was that of her niece, but she found the way it was written to be most unusual. She said it was as if the person who wrote the letter wanted to convince the family that it was authentic by mentioning the brand of cigarettes she smoked. "She said she quit smoking Marlboros," she stated. "I thought that was odd. If you quit smoking, you just say, 'I quit smoking.'"

Carlos Ibarra, who worked in the trailer park where Robinson lived, testified after Chidester that the defendant had asked him if his visiting mother, Lidia Ponce, could mail four or five pastel-colored letters upon her return home to Mexico in May 2000. In broken English, he explained that Robinson had told him he had a friend who was in hiding because she owed money to a bank and police were looking for her.

but she never would have gone off without calling home. I thought, 'Something is radically wrong here.' "

After she contacted police a short time later, they suggested she tape a call to Robinson, which she did on April 21, 2000, she said.

On the tape, which Morrison then played for the court, Robinson could be heard telling Carolyn that he had recently received a postcard from Suzette and Jim Turner saying they were off on an adventure. "I wouldn't get nervous," he told her. "From what I understand, they were on a boat somewhere. I thought they were going to Hawaii."

When Trouten told Robinson she was thinking of calling the police, he told her that her daughter "was a big girl." He also said that Jim Turner was a lawyer who was so rich he didn't need to work. "I really wouldn't worry," he reiterated.

Carolyn then lied and told Robinson she had received a doll from her daughter.

"You did?" he asked, sounding surprised.

"Yeah, but it was sent from Kansas City," she replied.

"Well, she mighta done that before she left here," he said. "When did you get this doll?

"Yesterday," Carolyn answered.

"When was it sent?"

"I didn't really pay any attention."

"What kind of doll are we talking about here?"

"Well, she's a Hawaiian doll. That's why I thought maybe that she had gotten back."

"Oh, no, no, no. From what I understand, they're not comin' back for . . . they're, they're going to sail around the world."

"You don't think I should notify someone?" Trouten asked him.

"Why?" he replied sharply, noting that he often didn't hear from his daughters for months when they traveled in Europe. "You know how young people are today."

The next morning, October 10, jurors watched the hotel

her he was the employer of the dogs' owner. They stayed, she said, until March 1, when the defendant picked them up by himself shortly after 2:00 P.M. and put them in a small carrier. "He was in a hurry," stated Cosby. "He seemed aggravated. He was angry that the bill was as much as it was. He said he had to get to the airport and he was rushing me."

As the court broke for lunch recess, ACO Rodney McClain was on the stand, testifying that he had been called to Santa Barbara Estates that same afternoon to pick up two strays. When he arrived about 2:35 P.M., he found two Pekingese dogs in a carrier in the front office, he said. They were later identified as Suzette's dogs.

Even Robinson's wife acknowledged that she remembered the dogs when the widely anticipated witness took the stand after lunch. Under initial questioning from Morrison, Nancy Robinson said that the clerk in her office, Alberta, had received a phone call from John about the stray Pekingese. "She turned around and said, 'Your husband is playing dog-catcher,'" testified Nancy, who was under subpoena to appear as a prosecution witness. "'He wants me to call the animal control officer.'"

Robinson, wearing a white pantsuit and blue top, also testified about the baby that her husband had brought home in January 1985. "She was dirty," his wife remembered, sighing heavily and trembling as she spoke. "She smelled. You just didn't hardly find dirt under a baby's fingernails."

Nancy stated that she bathed the baby, and her brother-in-law and his wife came to pick it up the next day. Morrison showed the court a family portrait that was taken at the reunion. In the photo, relatives surrounded a grinning Robinson, who had the baby seated on his lap.

"What was the baby's name?" asked Morrison.

"I think it was Tiffany," Nancy replied cautiously.

Asked by the prosecutor how she knew, Nancy said, "Because I was told."

"By who?" he asked.

"I would sure appreciate a glass of water," she replied sweetly. "Thank you."

With O'Brien's gentle guidance, she began to tell the court about her husband's obviously troubled relationships with most of his siblings and parents, by then both deceased. She described his oldest brother, Henry junior as a "very cruel person" who "walked off and left a wife with cancer and three children." John, she said, didn't have a relationship with him. He continued to be close to his sister, Joann, and had once been tight with his brother Donald. His sister Mary Ellen, she said distastefully, "was not very clean, weighs about three hundred pounds and never goes outside her house." His father, Henry senior, "worked the same place his whole life—Western Electric." His mother, she said, "was a very cold person" and the relationship had been strained for a long time before she passed away. "There really wasn't . . . [a relationship] after our first child," she stated. "I'd kind of force him to go up [to Chicago]. I finally quit doing that."

During O'Brien's cross-examination, Nancy said she knew her husband had had numerous affairs during their thirty-eight-year marriage. She was much more cooperative with the defense lawyer than she had been with the district attorney. She told the court she had asked her husband twice to move out. But both times she had taken him back. The second time was in late 1997 when she discovered he was having an affair with Izabela Lewicka, who was working for him on the magazine. "Probably in his briefcase, I saw a bank statement and a canceled check, where he was paying her rent," she stated, crying and dabbing at her eyes with Kleenex when asked how she knew. "Usually when I found out about [one of his affairs], it was over. This one wasn't. I truly thought he would probably leave me for her."

Robinson said she even visited an attorney about a divorce but didn't go through with it, largely because of her grand-daughter, who visited their house several times a week. "This

that would have been. "John would usually have dinner ready. I'm sure we had dinner."

"Why do you remember this day of all days?" asked O'Brien.

"Because of the dogcatcher thing," she replied, alluding to the animal control officer who had come to the mobile-home community that afternoon.

O'Brien gave the floor back to Morrison.

On redirect, the prosecutor asked Nancy why she had failed to mention the events of March 1, 2000, on two previous occasions when she had spoken to authorities and even during her testimony at the 2001 preliminary hearing. Authorities were alleging that Robinson had called her from the farm at 11:43 A.M. that morning, yet Nancy had just said she saw him about the same time with his grandkids in Olathe, roughly an hour away. He couldn't have been in both places at once.

Privately livid, Morrison believed she was lying on the stand in an attempt to offer an alibi for her husband on the very morning he murdered Suzette. State law, moreover, required defense attorneys to inform the prosecution in advance of any testimony that provided an alibi for the defendant. They hadn't done so.

"You said *nothing* about seeing your husband that morning!" Morrison thundered, apparently struggling to keep his anger in check.

"I guess, but I don't remember," replied the flustered witness before stepping down.

Detectives Lowther, Layman and Owsley spent what was left of Thursday afternoon and Friday, October 11, 2002, testifying about the treasure trove of items they found in Robinson's home and his Olathe storage locker, including sex toys, slave contracts, paperwork and personal effects connecting him to all six of his victims.

Their testimony laid the foundation for the disturbing evidence presented on Monday morning, October 14. The

"My what?"

"Your slut."

"Are you my slave?

"Yes, your slave."

"What does that mean, slave?"

"It means that I'm owned by you."

About this time, Robinson, naked, joined her. "Kiss your cock, bitch," he said.

She complied.

"What do you want your master to do to you, slut?" he asked.

"Anything he wants to," she replied.

"Do you know what it means to be a slave?" he asked. "You have no will of your own. You're totally owned by your master. Your body belongs to me, as evidenced by initials right there on my cheek. You're going to serve your master every morning . . . and every night."

He continued. "Your cock is your main concern. You will always please your cock. Do you understand?"

"Yes, master."

"Now I want you to get the Tens Unit set up. I want to see how this thing works while I drink my coffee."

As she obeyed him, Robinson used a whip to slap her several times on her backside. Suzette visibly cringed. "I just have a face thing," she explained.

"If I hit your face, it'll be with my hand, not with this," he told her sternly.

He sipped his coffee as she began to show him how to use the medical device to administer electrical shocks to her genitalia, jerking and jumping as he adjusted the pulse and frequency. "You've got to be an electrical engineer to use this thing," he said, seeming to grow bored.

He stretched out on his back. "Why don't you suck your cock, slut? Lick your balls, too. Do you like your balls, cunt?"

"Yes, master."

"Do you like the taste of your cock, the size of your cock? Do you like your master to face-fuck you often?"

Seconds later, Robinson was finished. "Now your master feels better," he said.

In the final scene, Suzette removed the three golf balls that Robinson had alluded to only moments before. Then the tape surreally cut away once again to Willy Wonka and the Chocolate Factory. Robinson had apparently recorded his sadomasochistic encounter over one of his grandkid's movies.

Some of the jurors were clearly uncomfortable, shifting in their seats as they watched the extremely graphic images flash before them on the screen. One middle-aged woman held her hand over her mouth throughout and briefly covered her eyes. Robinson sat with his chin in his right palm, nervously stroking his cheek with his index finger. But, as many in the courtroom noted, he watched every minute of the video, from beginning to end.

"Did he respond?" Welch asked.

"He had a very bad day, evidently," she replied. "He started cursing at me and told me I wasn't supposed to be in his blankety-blank barn and he would take care of my blankety-blank animals."

Welch asked the self-described devout woman if she could quote Robinson precisely.

"You want me to say curse words?" Grant asked.

Welch told Grant she thought this was one of those times when it would be okay to curse, causing several in the court-room to chuckle.

"I believe he started off with 'goddamn fucking neighbors' and 'fucking animals,' " Grant stated matter-of-factly. "Those were his best words."

Welch asked her if the man she saw that day was sitting in the courtroom. "Yes, ma'am," she replied, indicating the de-fendant. There was more laughter when she noted: "He's the one sitting there smiling."

"After the defendant yelled at you, what did you do?" Welch asked.

"I got down on my hands and my knees and went after my cat," she said. "I figured I was having a bad day, too."

Just then, one of her eight dogs, Montana, rushed into the barn and threw its body against her, Grant said. She started to scold the dog, she said, but then realized that Robinson was following her. "I just saw the shovel and the bottom of his boots," she said.

Managing to grab the cat, she headed outside as Montana continued to stay between her and Robinson. "I could hear him breathing really loud," she said. "I felt really bad I made him so mad. I kept apologizing all the way out of the barn."

Asked by defense attorney Sean O'Brien on cross-exami-nation if she recalled telling a detective that she had seen anguish in Robinson's eyes, Grant corrected him: "I didn't have a problem looking in his eyes and seeing great anger. There was no anguish."

Chapter 27

Dan Rundle, a forensic chemist with the Johnson County Crime Lab, followed Grant and other Linn County witnesses to the stand on Monday afternoon, October 14, 2002, to talk about the search for blood. The deputy said he and another crime lab analyst, Sally Lane, had been sent on March 29, 2000, to process the Guesthouse Suites hotel room where Suzette had stayed a month earlier. They detected several small reddish brown stains in the bathroom, on the curtains, on the bed and the mattress in the bedroom and in the living-room sofa bed. They also found a "fist-size" bloodstain on one of the sofa's seat cushions.

But while all that sounded promising—at least to some of those observing the testimony—Rundle said they could find no evidence of spatter patterns or drag marks and none of the stains they did discover were of evidentiary significance. "There were a lot of the typical stains you'd expect to find in a typical guestroom," he testified. "Nothing gave us any indication that anything really happened there."

Rundle, who returned to continue his testimony on Tuesday, October 15, said he and several other investigators from his crime lab were also assigned to look for blood, hair and skin in the three-bedroom trailer on Robinson's rural property. Beginning on June 3, 2000, and over the course of the next week, he said they found several items that tested positive for the presumptive presence of blood, including a wad of stained paper towels in the kitchen sink of Robinson's trailer. "It gave us a nice, good positive reaction," he testified,

Chapter 28

Izabela Lewicka's father took the stand on Tuesday and described his daughter as an independent and artistic young woman who insisted upon moving to Kansas in 1997 for what she called a summer "internship." Andrew Lewicki, who worked at Purdue University in West Lafayette, Indiana, said he couldn't get many details from his daughter. "She was very vague," admitted Lewicki, speaking with the thick accent of his native Poland. "All she told us was it was advertising for a small publisher. If she could find a good job after that, she might stay even longer."

Lewicki said Izabela had been born in Poland in April 1978 and was the older of his two daughters. Lewicki said he had moved to West Lafayette in 1988; his wife and daughters followed the next year. Graduating from Harrison High School in 1996, Izabela enrolled in Purdue's fine-arts program, taking drawing and painting courses, but continued to live at home.

Under cross-examination from O'Brien, Lewicki admitted that his daughter didn't appear to be happy in school and preferred to troll the Internet on their family computer at night. He said he didn't have access to her e-mail account and couldn't tell what Web sites she was visiting. "Izabela tended to keep to herself," he said. The art student was just finishing her freshman year, he added, when she suddenly announced her summer plans.

Lewicki and his wife both testified that they attempted to talk their daughter out of going, but they felt there wasn't a whole lot they could do. "She was past eighteen," explained

told her family she had gotten married. They invited her home several times, but she always refused, saying she was too busy. In the final months, she and her husband were always traveling in some exotic land, Lewicki said. Writing one of her last e-mails in the spring of 2000, she claimed to have just returned from a trip to China, he said.

Much like Carolyn Trouten had done, Izabela's mother also identified a number of items belonging to her daughter that had been found in Barbara Sandix's apartment—including a fiery Impressionistic painting, several pieces of clothing, the bedding she brought with her when she left Indiana, as well as a number of family heirlooms and books. "She used to read a lot of books," she testified.

On cross-examination, Marona-Lewicka acknowledged that they didn't know much about their daughter's move.

"Did she ever tell you the real reason she went to Kansas City?" O'Brien asked her gently.

"No," she said, her voice tinged with sadness. She stepped down.

But a friend from Lafayette, Indiana, acknowledged knowing much more. Jennifer Hayes said Izabela had confided that she was going to do secretarial work for an international publishing agent, who was also going to train her to become a BDSM dominatrix. However, Hayes said, she was going to start her education as his slave. "She wouldn't tell me anything other than he wanted her to call him master," testified Hayes, who said she had met Lewicka through friends at Purdue University. "She did call him John once."

Hayes said that Lewicka told her she was working on artwork for some BDSM manuscripts John had commissioned. She identified four photographs of her friend in different BDSM poses, which had been found in the defendant's Needmor Storage locker. She also identified two of the pencil drawings, which had been found in Barbara Sandre's duplex on Grant Avenue. She explained that Lewicka hadn't completed them when Hayes last saw her in spring 1997.

Chapter 29

Jurors were shown gruesome autopsy photographs of both Trouten and Lewicka as Donald Pojman, the deputy coroner, followed Hayes to the stand on Tuesday, October 15, to describe in detail how the two women had died. Pojman told the court that they arrived at the morgue still inside the eighty-five-gallon barrels that were discovered in the brush near a shed on Robinson's rural property. When he opened the barrels, they were curled up in the fetal position with their heads toward the bottom of the barrels, he said.

As color images were displayed on a screen in the courtroom, Pojman noted that Trouten was nude and wearing a blindfold tied around her head with a piece of soft nylon rope. Her nipples were pierced with rings that were connected by a chain, from which hung a butterfly pendant, he testified. She also had a number of other piercings in her ears and labia. The first injury on her "mildly" decomposed body, a small tear in the skin on the left side of her chest, was not serious enough to be lethal and was probably caused after her death, he said. Above her ear on the left side, however, a single blow had punched a circular hole in her skull more than an inch in diameter. "The young lady died shortly after receiving [this] injury," he testified.

Lewicka was nude except for a short-sleeved nightshirt. Her "moderately" decomposed body was partially covered by a greenish blue pillow, Pojman stated. He said he found a number of items, including several fingernails, three pieces of gray duct tape and two kitchen-size garbage bags, among the body fluids. Pojman said he believed Lewicka died from

Allen Hamm, who was promoted to assistant director of the Johnson County Crime Lab not long after the investigation, told the court he noticed several reddish brown stains on pieces of loose wallboard and molding when he was examining the south wall of the trailer's living room. Strands of hair mixed with what looked like human tissue were stuck to one of the boards. All of the spots, he testified before stepping down, tested positive for the presumptive presence of blood.

The months surrounding the trial had been a trying time for Roth and Welch. "Sara was in war mode for several months," the sergeant recalled. "There were all the motions filed by the defense and constant worry that something would go amiss. Flaws or oversights began to pop up here and there [and] was causing me quite a bit of anxiety. It seemed that all we talked about was the upcoming trial."

Once the trial started, the couple couldn't talk to each other about testimony because Roth was scheduled to testify. Of course, that was standard stuff at trials. The detectives couldn't talk to each other, either. But Welch and Roth were both concerned that the defense might try to make an issue out of the fact that they were dating. So, once the trial began, they kept their conversations very vague—when they saw each other at all. "I was constantly at work," Welch said. "When I wasn't at work, I was sleeping. Rick had to start taking care of my dry cleaning because I got to the office before the dry cleaners opened and I left the office after it was closed! I have never worked so hard in my life. I digress."

For Welch, not talking about the trial was less of a problem than she anticipated. What was difficult was if one of Roth's detectives did well or poorly on the stand, that's all she could say. Or if a witness said something funny, she could not tell him. "I never had a clue what she was talking about," Roth said. "I had to get my news like everyone else the next day. Then I could usually piece together who so-and-so was and

"When they popped the lid on the first barrel," Roth replied. "It was horrendous."

"You saw [the reddish] liquid and did not smell a thing?" Berrigan, on recross, asked incredulously.

"I did not smell a thing," Roth insisted.

Morrison next called Johnson County detective Harold Hughes to the stand, who testified that he had been examining the trailer on Robinson's rural property when another investigator informed him that a cadaver dog had focused on some barrels out by the toolshed. He went to investigate and found one of the yellow metal barrels standing upright near a shed on the property, he stated.

Hughes told how he used pliers to loosen the bolt on the seal of the first yellow barrel and popped the lid to look inside. He said he repeated the same procedure with the second yellow barrel. "I opened the barrels and determined there was a body in each barrel," he testified.

At this point, Morrison asked him to identify the two yellow barrels that had been rolled into the courtroom. Hughes confirmed that they were the same yellow barrels from that fateful day, but he added that they looked considerably different since they had been cleaned. Morrison, who had also set up a VCR in the courtroom, played a clip that showed Hughes opening the second yellow drum and a glimpse at what was inside: a bluish-green pillow partially covering the back of a body that was curled up in a fetal position.

"Did you smell anything?" asked Morrison.

"I could smell it as I walked up to it," replied Hughes.

Opening the lid to the first barrel, the clip showed another body slumped over in a similar manner.

The jury, which by now had viewed graphic autopsy photos and a sex tape, did not visibly react to the tape of the crime scene. Robinson appeared to be watching, tilting his head in the direction of the screen.

box at the Overland Park business. Lewicka's name was on the agreement, she noted, along with that of another woman. When it was updated in 1999, the paperwork indicated that John Robinson had added his name to the list of those persons eligible to receive mail, she said.

A second friend of Lewicka's took the stand to talk about what she knew of her decision to move to Kansas City. Dawn Carter of Columbus, Ohio, who met Lewicka in a dance class at Purdue University in August 1996, said her friend had a key to her apartment and often stayed with her or came over during the day just to hang out or use her computer.

ADA Welch asked Carter, a thirty-one-year-old graduate student with cropped blond hair, if she was aware of other interests that Lewicka had. "She loved art," she said. "She took sketchbooks with her everywhere she went. She also liked purple ink. If she was writing a note to say she'd be home at seven-thirty, she would write it out in ink and decorate it."

In the spring of 1997, Lewicka told her she was going to move to Kansas City and get a job, Carter said. She also had plans of hopefully traveling, she testified. "She talked about John, a guy she met on the Internet," she said. "She said that John was helping her to get set up and helping her to get an apartment."

Carter said they had a little argument because she didn't think Lewicka should go, and so Lewicka put her on the phone to talk with John.

"What did you talk about?" asked Welch.

"Silly things," she replied. "I think she told him I collected fountain pens. He said he had a big collection. He had a dragon pen. He said he cared about her. He said she had a lot of talent. He said he wanted to help her."

But when Carter told him she didn't trust him, he appeared threatened by that, she said. "Izabela took the phone," she testified.

Lewicka also showed her an e-mail that John had sent. "We were having a conversation about her sex life and things she

Chapter 31

Barbara Sandre followed Carter to the stand that Wednesday afternoon, testifying that she was a German translator who had met the defendant nearly thirty years earlier when he had come to Toronto to see the Boy Scout production she was involved in. They struck up a pen pal relationship but eventually lost touch, the heavyset woman with short blond hair and glasses recalled.

They were back in touch again around 1971, when their friendship turned romantic. But after he paid her a brief visit, she didn't hear from him again until 1993. Out of the blue, Sandre said, her parents received a letter purportedly from John Robinson's "adopted son." They forwarded it to her in England, where she was then residing.

At this point in Sandre's testimony, the prosecution attempted to submit the letter as evidence, but O'Brien called for a bench conference and, within seconds, the jury was ushered out. Welch explained that they wanted to submit the letter to show a pattern of conduct in Robinson's regular use of forged letters. She also pointed out that Nancy Robinson had found the letter and it was what prompted her to write Sandre, as she had mentioned in her testimony. But O'Brien said the letter was immaterial and didn't make any difference why or how Robinson rekindled his relationship with Sandre. Without explaining his rationale, the judge sided with the defense, refusing to allow the letter.

With the jury reseated, Sandre testified that she had responded to the note, sending her reply to one of Robinson's

"What were their names?" asked Welch.

"John junior, Chris, Chrissy and Kimberly," Sandre replied.

"Did you meet any of these children?" Welch asked.

"No," she replied.

"Go to their homes?" she continued.

"No," she repeated.

In late August 1999, Sandre moved to an unfurnished apartment on Grant Avenue in Overland Park, signing a lease with John Robinson. "He said he had furniture in storage that I could use," Sandre testified, adding that Robinson paid for her move with a Specialty Publications check and soon arrived with another moving truck full of furniture.

Upon further questioning, she recalled that the name of the moving company was something like Two Men and a Truck.

By the end of the month, he had also arrived with a host of other items, she said, including artwork, bedding, towels, dishes, pots and pans and cutlery. "He told me he had bought the older things from estate sales and that some things were his grandmother's," Sandre said.

The Canadian woman then identified several items as among those that Robinson had brought over. They included a fiery Impressionistic painting that was hung in her living room and was signed "John 1992." Two pencil drawings also had his signature and initials with the year 2000. Only the day before, her mother and friend had identified the paintings and drawings as having been done by Izabela Lewicka.

Sandre, moreover, identified the bluish green Aztec-printed sheets that she said had come from Robinson, which matched the pillowcase found in the barrel with Lewicka's body. "I had an almost brand new and large garbage can that I packed all my bedding in so they wouldn't get damp and musty and dirty," Sandre stated. "These things were all standing in the dining room in readiness to go to storage or be packed away or whatever . . . I don't believe there were any pillowcases, to my recollection."

"When the defendant brought [the Aztec-printed sheets]

When Robinson wanted something, he didn't take no for an answer, she added.

Resuming her testimony the next morning, on Thursday, October 17, Sandre relayed several more incidents in which Robinson misled her about his marital status.

She was living in England in 1998 when she received a letter signed by a woman named Nancy Robinson, who claimed she was Robinson's wife.

"Were you aware of her existence prior to receiving this letter?" asked Welch.

"No," she replied.

"Had you heard the name Nancy Robinson before?"

"Never."

Sandre testified that she immediately sent John Robinson an e-mail, saying she had just received a letter from his wife. "He e-mailed me back and said, 'What wife?' she said.

After Sandre faxed John Robinson the letter, she received an explanation that apparently satisfied her.

"He said that she was someone he had hired when his kids were little when he was working and she was now working for his daughter baby-sitting her children, and that he, after I had given him the letter, had been to a lawyer and had gotten a court order so that she couldn't harass anybody in his family anymore."

In October 1999, Sandre went to Sam's Club with a friend who had a store membership. "We're pushing the trolley around on one particular row," said Sandre. "I'm going down the row and I think to myself, 'That looks like J.R. coming towards me. So I got a little bit closer and I think I actually almost rolled over his toe. He looked right through me like he had never seen me before in his life."

Robinson was with a woman who looked older, Sandre said. The woman had grayish hair and wore glasses. When Sandre got home that evening, she e-mailed Robinson to say she had seen him at the store with another woman.

Chapter 32

That Thursday afternoon, October 17, prosecutors paraded several more witnesses through the courtroom to testify about Lewicka's relationship with Robinson. Robert Meyers, owner of A. Friendly's Bookstore, in Overland Park, said Lewicka was a regular customer from 1997 to 1999. Her main interests were books about the occult, vampires, sorcery, witchcraft and historic events, such as the Salem witch trials. She spoke with an Eastern European accent and often dressed in dark clothing, Meyers said. "She would come in maybe once a month for two years or more," he said.

Most of the time, Lewicka came in alone, Meyers said. But on one of her last visits, around August 1999, an older man who looked about fifty-three years of age and was "somewhat corpulent" accompanied her into the store. Meyers said the visit stood out because Lewicka was wearing a black dog collar with silver studs and announced to him that she was moving. In the future, the man with her would be shopping for her books, she told Meyers. "He seemed to be disinterested," Meyers said in describing the man's reaction to Izabela's comments, adding that he never saw the man again. "I believe very possibly he's the defendant."

Karen Scott, a print broker for Robinson's magazine, *Manufactured Modular Home Living,* testified that the defendant told her Lewicka was his adopted daughter. Izabela worked with Robinson as a graphic designer in 1998 and for most of 1999, she said. But that had changed in September 1999 when Robinson called Scott, seeking names of people

Julie Brown, an employee with the property management company, testified that Robinson had rented the apartment for Lewicka in January 1999 but broke the one-year lease early in September. Inspecting the apartment after it had been vacated, Brown found that the kitchen and front room were not terribly clean, while the two bedrooms were immaculate and looked as though they'd recently been repainted. "It looked like someone . . . sucked all the dirt out of the area, it was so clean," she testified.

Brian Palmeter, vice president of daily operations at Two Men and a Truck, followed Brown to the stand. He told the court that on August 23, 1999, Robinson called them to move a few belongings from Izabela's Edgebrook apartment to Sandre's duplex on Grant Avenue.

Welch asked Palmeter to examine and explain the company's "move sheet."

"Just looking at this information, I would have to guess the contact person was probably the one that called it in," Palmeter stated.

"That's John Robinson?" Welch asked.

"Yes," he replied.

"This would be the move to Grant Avenue?"

"That's the information that was given to us at the time of the scheduling."

"The date would be 8/23/99?"

"Yes, ma'am."

Welch said she had no further questions for Palmeter and moved to her next witness: Johnson County crime scene analyst Sally Lane.

Obtaining a search warrant for the apartment more than a year after Lewicka vacated, Lane said she focused on the doors, flooring, carpeting and walls because other tenants had since occupied the apartment. In the southwest bedroom, she hit pay dirt: discovering what appeared to be hundreds of pin-size blood specks sprayed on two walls and a set of window blinds. "The majority of them were from waist to chest high,"

hairs from either the paper towel or wallboard could have belonged to Robinson, Booth said his tests were conclusive. "It's
not his hair," he testified.

Booth also said the swabs taken from a yellow pickup
truck and from inside a pole barn on the property did not
contain blood. Neither did the nine hammers, two picks
and a chisel seized in the mobile home. The mystery of the
missing murder weapon would remain unsolved.

Finally Morrison shifted his questioning to Izabela's apartment, where crime lab technicians had taken the swabs of
stains from two walls in the south bedroom and one swab
from window blinds. The blinds quickly were ruled out as
having stains of significance. "It was definitely not blood,"
Booth said. "It was like a soft drink had exploded."

But all six swabs taken from bedroom walls tested positive
as being human blood, Booth said.

Morrison asked whose blood it was.

There was a pregnant pause in the courtroom as observers
strained their ears to hear Booth's answer. They needn't have
bothered.

"Izabela Lewicka," he crowed triumphantly.

The blood evidence supported the prosecution's theory that
the twenty-one-year-old Indiana art student had been killed
in her apartment and her body somehow transported to the
farm.

"How did you treat him?" Morrison asked.

"As best I could," she replied.

Robinson wanted sex often and he would usually come to her apartment to get it, she testified. Later on in the course of their two-year relationship, they would meet at other locations. Under further questioning, she insisted they had a normal sexual relationship, although from her descriptions it sounded as if he at least tried to introduce aspects of BDSM. He always wanted oral sex, she testified, and also had a leather collar with restraints for her hands, which he had tried on her one time. He took pictures of her getting undressed and later made a video, she said. "He would sometimes call me his personal slut and whore," she said. "Not really during sex but during foreplay—to try to put me in my place."

At one point during their relationship, she was working part-time at an athletic club and he took a black Magic Marker and wrote his initials on her hip. "He wanted to know if I got undressed in the locker room," she testified. "When I said yes, he said he wanted to me wear his initials so everybody could see."

In the fall of 1998, Robinson told Cox he needed to do some traveling for his business, she testified, and he wanted her to go with him to London, Paris and Australia. At his suggestion, she gave up her job and her apartment, moved her furniture and belongings into storage, and applied for a passport. Morrison asked her how long the trip was supposed to last. "About six weeks," she said. "I asked him [about that] several times because my family was curious and I didn't get a straight answer until I pushed and then he was still vague."

Before they left, he had her prepare several letters in advance to her mother and young daughter, pretending she was in places such as London and Paris, she said.

"Did he say why he wanted you to write these letters?" Morrison asked.

"I asked [him] because I thought it was rather odd," she replied. "He said we wouldn't have enough time to write. I

she said, emphasizing that they never had a master/slave relationship.

"Did you take this thing seriously or not?" Morrison asked, referring to the slave contract. "No," she answered.

Sometime later that year, she recalled Robinson showing her an apartment he said he owned on Edgebrook. She remembered seeing boxes, clothing, a computer and miscellaneous items. She said Robinson asked her if she wanted to live in the apartment, but she declined. He also asked her if she wanted any of the clothing and she accepted a few garments. She identified the garments—including a green velour dress, a black velour sweater and a white silk camisole—in court that afternoon. They were the same items of clothing that Izabela's mother had identified only three days before as belonging to her daughter.

Cox also said she paid a visit to an apartment on Grant Avenue. Robinson told her that a woman he knew from London was using it and would be back soon. In the meantime, he said, she could stay there since she was living out of her car. She stayed two or three nights, she said.

The witness also admitted to Morrison that she had signed paperwork giving power of attorney to Robinson on July 13, 1999. "It was his idea," she said. Morrison asked her to identify another item that had been found in Robinson's black hardcover case in the Needmor Storage locker. It was the title to her car, a 1986 Chevy Cavalier. She didn't know why he had it.

Finally Morrison asked her if she'd ever been to the defendant's farm. He had talked about it, she said, but they never visited. "He said we'd have sex and lots of it," she testified. "He said he would like to tie me up in the barn and have sex with me and leave and come back whenever he chose and fuck me some more."

On cross-examination, Berrigan asked Cox if Robinson had ever hurt or threatened her. "He did hurt me once when he tried to put nipple clips on me," she said, though she admitted that the relationship was consensual.

Chapter 34

Prosecutors had spent nearly two weeks calling more than sixty witnesses to take the stand to testify about Trouten and Lewicka. Returning from morning recess on Friday, October 18, however, they finally moved fifteen years back in time to focus on Robinson's third alleged murder victim in the Kansas trial: Lisa Stasi.

Karen Gaddis, the former ob-gyn social worker at Truman Medical Center in Independence, Missouri, a hospital well known for its care of the indigent, kicked off testimony about Stasi by describing the1980s as lean years for social-service agencies, forcing them to think outside the box to solve problems. She said it was in this context that Robinson called her in December 1984 and purported to be a businessman who wanted to give back to the community. He told her he had formed an organization to help needy young mothers. But Robinson never produced any paperwork regarding his purported venture. "It made us feel somewhat uneasy," she testified.

Robinson specifically said he was looking for white women in their late teens or early twenties who were pregnant or had newborn babies, Gaddis said. He also said he was looking for women who did not have strong family ties in the area because they would be most in need of his help.

"Did that raise a red flag?" asked Morrison.

"It did," she said.

Contradicting what she had told Overland Park detectives and probation officer Stephen Haymes more than fifteen

were going to help her find a job and earn her GED and that a man named John Osborne was spearheading the effort.

While Lisa went out that evening to a local bar called The Log Cabin, Klinginsmith said she looked after four-month-old Tiffany. "I fed her; she slept a long time; she took a bubble bath," stated Klinginsmith, who testified that she became a little upset when it grew late and Lisa hadn't returned. Klinginsmith called her brother, John Stasi, and he fetched Lisa from the bar and brought her to his parents' house to spend the night.

Returning to Klinginsmith's home the next morning, Lisa told her sister-in-law that Osborne was putting her up in room 131 at the Rodeway Inn in Overland Park and that they had tickets to go to Chicago.

"Did you give her any advice?" asked Morrison.

"Yes, I did," Klinginsmith replied. "I told her she ought to be cautious because, for one, she didn't know him that well. She didn't know what his intentions were."

But Lisa Stasi replied that Osborne was looking for her and that she had left a message with the Rodeway Inn for him to call. The phone rang a few minutes later and Klinginsmith wound up giving Osborne directions to her house. "He came to the door about twenty-five minutes later, rang the door-bell," said Klinginsmith, who noted that he'd traveled through a bad snowstorm to get there. "I went to the door with my son, who was five, and Lisa put on her coat."

He seemed like he was in a hurry and didn't waste any time on pleasantries. "He didn't say anything to me," Klinginsmith stated. "He just stood there and looked at me."

Morrison asked her if she recognized the man in court who had called himself John Osborne. "Yes," she replied.

She indicated the defendant.

Lisa carried Tiffany to Osborne's car, which was parked down the street, leaving her own yellow Toyota Corolla and many of her belongings behind, Klinginsmith continued. The young mother called about an hour later to let her sister-in-law

That was the last time she spoke to Lisa, Betty Stasi testified. Within a few weeks, however, she received a typed letter with Lisa's signature at the bottom.

Welch asked her about the contents of the letter. "She said she was going out of town somewhere and she was going to start a new life for her and Tiffany," she stated.

Also testifying on that Friday, October 18, was Cindy Scott, the former Overland Park detective who had originally investigated Lisa and Tiffany's disappearance. She told the court that part of her job was to determine whether the individuals in question had met foul play or simply wanted to be left alone. She said she was aware right from the beginning that Lisa's family was suspicious about John Robinson. "Some of Lisa Stasi's family had concerns," she stated. "They knew she left with Mr. Robinson."

Scott said she had questioned Robinson almost immediately, along with numerous members of Lisa and Tiffany's family. He told her that he was trying to help Stasi as part of his program for young mothers, but she had changed her mind, Scott testified. She said Robinson told her that Stasi came to his office to thank him and left with her baby and a young man. "He hadn't heard from her since then," she stated, adding that he also told her he didn't ask Lisa to sign any papers.

Stephen Haymes, called to the stand next, had to be careful not to make any mention of Robinson's criminal record, lest prosecutors risk a mistrial. He testified that he, too, had questioned the defendant about his connection to Stasi, though the jury was never told that Haymes was Robinson's old probation supervisor. Again Robinson said he had put Stasi up at the Overland Park motel, but she had changed her mind about the program, Haymes testified. Robinson said Lisa Stasi was with a man named Bill and was going to Colorado.

In March, however, Haymes said Robinson told him another story. "He told me that Lisa and the baby had been found in the Kansas City area," Haymes stated. Lisa, with Tiffany in tow, had apparently done some recent baby-sitting

adoptions and he'd get in touch with him for us," said Don Robinson.

In early 1984, the defendant called to let the couple know that an attorney by the name of Doug Wood was willing to work with them and that a baby should be ready in October. But, Don Robinson said, his brother also explained that he would serve as the go-between for them and the attorney because "Doug wasn't very easy to get along with."

At that point, the Robinsons borrowed $2,500 and wrote out a cashier's check to Equi-II, Robinson's business, to start the adoption process. The couple also fixed up a room in their house for the baby and put a crib on layaway. In September, Frieda quit her job at Ace Hardware in anticipation of the baby's arrival.

Don Robinson said he never met Wood but that the attorney had called him once. "I did talk to somebody one time who said he was Doug Wood," he stated. But October came and went with no news about a baby. "I don't remember the exact reasons, but it fell through," stated Frieda, who took the stand immediately after her husband.

Then, in early January 1985, his older brother called, Don said. He said a baby girl was available and they should come quickly to Kansas City to pick her up. The baby's mother had wanted to give her up for adoption when she was born, the defendant said, but a social worker had talked her out of it. Disowned by her family, the young mother left her baby in a shelter, checked into a hotel and killed herself.

Don Robinson said he and his wife flew from Chicago to Kansas City to pick up their baby daughter on January 10, 1985. His brother met them at the airport and drove them to the offices of Equi-II, where they signed what they thought were official adoption papers and gave him a second $3,000 check made out to Wood. In return, Don Robinson said his brother handed them a wallet-size photo of their new baby daughter. In court, Don Robinson identified a photo of his

wrenching discovery. She was wearing the same outfit as the missing baby, Frieda said, and both pictures appeared to be a part of the same series.

A fingerprint examiner followed the Robinsons to the stand on Monday to confirm briefly that prints taken from Tiffany Stasi at the time of her birth in September 1984 matched those of Heather Robinson. Three other witnesses—including a district judge, Ron Wood, (Robinson's old attorney) and another attorney, Doug Wood—also testified that their signatures on Heather Robinson's adoption papers had been forged.

While Doug Wood, who at the time of the trial was up for reelection as Johnson County commissioner, had briefly rented office space to Robinson, he stressed that he had never helped him with any adoptions or accepted any money.

A fourth witness told the court that she had been Robinson's BDSM mistress in the mid-1980s and signed blank sheets of paper at his request. Even though a notary public stamp and her signature, Evi Gresham, appeared on the adoption papers, the woman insisted that she had never been a notary public and had never seen the papers until authorities showed them to her after Robinson's arrest.

The testimony about Lisa Stasi and her four-month-old baby prompted lively discussion on Court TV's Web site, which was covering the case. One young woman, writing under the moniker of 'LoveConquersAll,' first chimed in on Oct. 12, complaining about the media coverage. "I won't lie and say it isn't interesting because it is," she wrote on a message board devoted to the Robinson trial. "But these people have suffered enough. How much more must they suffer because of our curiosity? And it is sad that the victims are labeled "The Missing Baby" and "The Brother" and so forth. I am sure the poor child does not need to hear that. [She] must have been traumatically affected from this. The loving family that took good care of her was betrayed as well. I believe they

Chapter 35

Nearing the homestretch of the prosecution's case, DA Morrison called several witnesses on Tuesday, October 22, 2002, to testify about the two women and teenage girl discovered in Robinson's Missouri storage locker.

Dr. Thomas Young, the Jackson County coroner, who testified that the murderer had wielded a blunt object, like a hammer to kill the three females with several powerful blows to the head. One of the women, he said, forty-five-year-old Sheila Faith, also had a fracture on her right forearm that was consistent with a defensive injury. Judging by the advanced state of decomposition, Young said, all three could have been dead five or six years.

Next up was Beverly Bonner's younger brother, Larry Heath, who described a series of letters he had received from his dead sister beginning in January 1994. In the first one, a recently divorced Bonner wrote in her own hand, he said, that she had taken a new job in the human resources department of a large international corporation and would be training in Chicago and then traveling extensively throughout Europe. She told him to write her at a mailbox facility in Olathe, Kansas, which would forward her correspondence to wherever she was stationed. Her next letter, which arrived in April 1994, and all subsequent letters were typewritten, he said, and in them she described working closely with new boss "Jim Redmond" as they circled the globe.

Heath, a bald and bearded truck driver from Florida, identified thirteen letters that his sister had sent to him from

Olathe, followed Beverly's brothers to the stand, testifying that the defendant, using the name James Turner, had rented a mailbox for Beverly Jean Bonner in 1994. "He told me she was working for him and was going to be going to Australia and he was going to take care of her mail," she testified, explaining that Robinson had provided copies of Bonner's identification to open the mailbox.

Robinson rented a second mailbox in June 1994 for Sheila and Debbie Faith, Davis said. "Mr. Turner picked up mail at least once a month," she said, still referring to him by his alias. "He received two government checks monthly in the names of Sheila Faith and Debbie Faith."

Davis testified that she never saw anyone collect the checks except Robinson.

"How long did he receive them?" Welch asked.

"It would have been June [2000] because they were still sitting here when Mr. Turner was arrested," she replied.

On cross-examination, Pat Berrigan questioned Davis's ability to remember just who had rented the mailboxes, since it was so many years ago and she had many patrons. But she stuck to her story. "In my business, we try to remember our customers and to speak to them on a regular basis," she said firmly.

Two of Sheila Faith's sisters then took the stand, saying they had begun to receive typewritten letters from their sister and niece not long after they disappeared in the summer of 1994. "She always handwrote her letters," said her sister Kathy Norman, who received letters postmarked from Canada and the Netherlands. "This isn't Sheila," testified her other sister, Michelle Fox, referring to a letter she received from her sister in 1995. "It was happy. Sheila wasn't a happy person."

Perhaps the most compelling testimony about the Faiths, however, came from a close friend from Pueblo, Colorado, who described how the lonely widow left Colorado with her teenage daughter, never to return. "Sheila and I were as close as sisters could be," said Nancy Guerrero, who met her friend in Santa Ana, California, when both of their daughters

break for the day because prosecutors had failed to include her on their witness list and O'Brien and Berrigan were in the dark as to who she was. "Neither Mr. O'Brien nor I have ever heard of this woman in our lives," Berrigan stated. "I just wrote him a note, 'Who is this woman?' "

Returning to the stand on Wednesday morning, October 23, Shields explained that Robinson—using the alias "BJ Bonner"—had hired her as a researcher for his company, Specialty Publications, but that their relationship primarily consisted of BDSM sex sessions at her apartment. At one point, he told her that his sister had died and brought over several items that he said came from her storage locker. Among the items he gave her, Shields said, was an angel cross-stitch encased in a gold frame. She said it was hanging on her wall when the news broke about Robinson's arrest.

Beverly Brewington, senior vice president of the Community Bank of Raymore, then testified that a James Turner and Beverly Bonner had opened up a business account at her bank under the name of Hydro-Gro, in February 1994. She also said that the account holders had cashed Social Security checks made out to the Faiths and deposited them into the business account from July 1994 to September 1995. In the fall of 1995, Brewington's bank sent a notice to Turner and Bonner, saying that they could no longer deposit personal checks into a business account, she said. There was no further activity on the account, she noted. But Bret Manz, a Bank of America supervisor, testified that Social Security checks made out to the Faiths had also been deposited more recently into a business account at his bank. The account was for Specialty Publications of America, Inc., d.b.a. Manufactured Modular Home Living.

Beverly Bonner's ex-husband also took the stand on Wednesday, testifying that he last saw her in court when their divorce was finalized around February 1994. At that time, their house had been sold and she was in the process of moving to Raymore, Missouri, Dr. William Bonner said. She told him she was taking a job with a company out of Chicago that involved world

"No, sir."

"If I told you that Mr. Robinson was incarcerated because he violated probation for stealing out of Clay County, would you have a quarrel with that?" Berrigan followed.

"The only thing we ever had access to was medical records," Bonner replied. "I had no information to the contrary."

The brief exchange marked the first and only time that jurors would hear testimony about Robinson's prior criminal record.

R.E. Holtz, a special agent for the Social Security Administration, told the court that in 1993 his agency had been sending monthly survivor benefit checks to Faith and her daughter in Colorado after her husband died of cancer. But in June 1994, they began sending them to a post office box in Olathe, he said.

"How does one go about changing one's address?" Morrison asked the witness.

"By telephone or by letter," replied Holtz, who identified about 150 Social Security checks worth more than $80,000 that had been cashed between June 1994 and June 2000, when Robinson was arrested.

Latent-print examiner Lyla Thompson took the stand that Wednesday afternoon, October 23, testifying that she found Robinson's fingerprints on several glass items that belonged to Suzette Trouten packed in a box in his rural trailer. Thompson also noted that a fingerprint on a bloodstained roll of duct tape did not match Robinson's prints or those of the law officers who had handled it. Earlier DNA testimony matched the blood on the tape to Lewicka, but Thompson said she could not compare the fingerprint on the tape with Lewicka's because the young woman's body had been too decomposed to obtain "known" prints.

Returning to the stand on Thursday morning, October 24, Thompson revealed a couple of surprises. Robinson's fingerprints, she testified, were all over several of the Faiths' Social Security checks—further proof that the defendant had picked up the checks at the Mailroom and cashed them in two local

Chapter 36

Vickie Neufeld was the prosecution's last witness, taking the stand for more than an hour on Thursday afternoon, October 24. The psychologist broke down as she described her sexual encounters with Robinson. "'This is how we find out if we have chemistry,'" she quoted the defendant as saying as he took off his clothes, stretched out on the bed and demanded oral sex. When she complied, he pulled out a camera and started taking pictures of her, she said. "I didn't want him to do that," she testified, softly crying. He then moved to a chair, took her by the hair and pulled her to her knees in front of him. Still gripping her hair, she said, "he thrust himself in [my mouth] and thrust my head back and forth until he ejaculated."

As Neufeld testified, Robinson's daughter Christy Shipps sat in the front row of the courtroom gallery, her hand covering her mouth. At one point, John Robinson glanced back at his daughter, gave her a little smile and shook his head, as if to say he couldn't believe what the witness was telling the court about him. With tears in her eyes, she managed to smile back.

Robinson, Vickie continued, returned to her hotel room the next day. This time, she testified that he grew angry when she didn't take off her clothes quickly enough. He yanked her sweater off and demanded she take off the rest, she said. He then put around her neck a leather collar that was attached to handcuffs he fastened to her wrists. She told him the collar was too tight, she said. "I was afraid," she testified. "In BDSM, you have role-playing. But you also have negotiation."

hundred pieces of evidence and dozens of photos. Despite Neufeld's testimony that she did not consent, the judge ruled that there was not enough evidence to support a criminal charge of sexual battery. "Frankly, the evidence at the preliminary hearing was borderline," he said dismissing the charge. "If anything, it got thinner here."

However, he let stand the charge in which Neufeld claimed Robinson had stolen about $700 worth of her sex toys.

After only a short break, the defense called its first witness, Marsha Keylon, another housekeeper at the Guesthouse Suites. Keylon briefly testified that she saw Suzette only three times during her evening shift at the Lenexa hotel. Twice she was alone. The third meeting was as Suzette entered her suite with a man in his thirties not fitting Robinson's description.

Suzette's former employer, Sharon LaPrad, was their second witness and she wasn't on the witness stand much longer than Keylon. Suzette had worked for her off and on for nine years in Monroe, Michigan, before leaving to take a job in Kansas she stated. LaPrad cautioned her about taking the job, presumably to care for Robinson's elderly father. The job was to involve world travel and a $60,000 salary. "I just thought it was too good to be true," LaPrad told the court.

Suzette's landlord and friend from Monroe, Michigan, testified that she had given him a different reason for moving to Kansas City. Trouten said she had cancer and was going to an oncology clinic, John Stapleton said. She was also going to apply for welfare assistance, Stapleton said, and she told him it was easier to obtain in Kansas. She would then send him the $1,200 she owed him for rent and telephone bills. Before stepping down, Stapleton said he later learned from Lore Remington and Carolyn Trouten that he had "been told an out-and-out lie."

After Stapleton's testimony, Berrigan told the court that the defense had no other witnesses for the day but would return with "somebody" the next morning, Friday, October 25.

However, when morning came—and after a couple of

Chapter 37

In his closing remarks on Monday morning, October 28, Paul Morrison called the defendant a "sinister" man who for years had lured women to their deaths and gone to great lengths to conceal his crimes. "There is one common thread between all of these women and that one common thread is John Robinson," he told a courtroom filled to capacity, which once again included the relatives of several victims and Robinson's wife and daughter. "When we're done [with our closing arguments], we will prove this case not only beyond a reasonable doubt but beyond any doubt."

Morrison told jurors that Robinson had lured Suzette Trouten from Michigan not only to take part in a sex and bondage relationship but with the promise of a $60,000 job and world travel. "Do you think she would have willingly come down to Lenexa, Kansas, to be murdered?" he asked. "The defendant sold her a bill of goods, like he's sold so many others a bill of goods."

He described how, in one e-mail, Trouten had fantasized about being blindfolded and taken to some rural area to service her master. "Perhaps that's why she was blindfolded," the prosecutor said. "Perhaps that's why she was nude" when her body was found in the barrel.

Referring to the thirty-nine-minute videotape of the two having sadomasochistic sex, he said the words were almost as disturbing as the images on the screen. "He thought he owned her—but it got old," he argued. Trouten, he said, wanted a full-time relationship with Robinson and that was pretty hard

town at the same time that Lewicka disappears, Morrison said. Robinson moves the woman, a Canadian named Barbara Sandre, into an apartment and brings over furniture, bedding, books and a fiery Impressionistic painting. "Lewicka died so his new girlfriend could have furniture," Morrison argued.

The prosecutor said he also believed that Robinson killed Lewicka in the apartment he had rented for her, noting that hundreds of pin-size spots of her blood were sprayed on the bedroom wall. Lewicka's body was clothed in a nightshirt and covered by a pillow in the barrel, Morrison said. "It was as if she were sleeping in the bedroom when she was killed," he stated.

Shifting back in time, he described how Robinson was under pressure in the mid-1980s to find a baby for his brother and sister-in-law to adopt. He said the defendant contacted social-service agencies looking for white girls with babies, preferably those who didn't have strong family ties. "Do you think it's because no one will be looking for them?" he asked.

Lisa Stasi and her baby met that description, Morrison said, noting that Kathy Klinginsmith, her sister-in-law, had testified that Robinson came to collect Stasi and her baby from her house on January 9, 1985. Because there was a snowstorm, he said, Stasi called Klinginsmith when she got back to her room at the Rodeway Inn to let her know she had arrived safely. She called her mother-in-law a little later and this time she was hysterical. Morrison quoted her as saying, " 'They want me to sign papers. They're coming to take my baby.' "

Morrison maintained, "That's the only evidence of any-body else being remotely involved in these crimes."

He said Robinson's brother and sister-in-law showed up the next day to adopt their baby. Morrison showed one of the photos they took that day to the jurors. "There he is, grinning like a Cheshire cat, within hours of Lisa Stasi having that baby ripped from her arms," Morrison said. "It's the same old story—just a different year."

Defense attorney Sean O'Brien, however, insisted that the

O'Brien also said that Robinson's admitted relationship with all of these women did not mean he killed them. "He's directly connected to these women, but he's not connected to the violence," he argued. He added that Robinson's wife and brother, the two people who were closest to him, had expressed shock and disbelief upon learning that he'd been arrested. "'I thought I was going to pass out,'" he quoted Nancy as testifying.

O'Brien also said that the physical evidence raised a lot of unanswered questions and suggested that more than one person committed the crimes. He argued that the barrels were too heavy to be lifted by one person. He cited the mysterious fingerprint on a roll of duct tape that contained a smudge of Lewicka's blood, which did not belong to Robinson. And he said that there was a palm print on the plastic wrapping two of the barrels in the Missouri locker that also did not belong to him. "Maybe in ten, fifteen years, we'll find out who [those prints] belong to and it will make us look at this case in a very different light," he said.

After the court heard from O'Brien, Paul Morrison came back to deliver his rebuttal. "Before we spend a lot of time talking about the fingerprint on the duct tape or why there were no letters from Izabela, let's think about the fact that those barrels with those bodies are on *his* farm," he thundered. "The defense is saying, 'Look at all the questions.' Over seventeen years, that's the best that they can come up with? I think you'll find that there are very few unanswered questions. The evidence in this case is overwhelming."

Morrison acknowledged that there was an unidentifiable fingerprint on the duct tape. However, he said, that didn't mean it wasn't Lewicka's and, in fact, he thought that it probably was. "We don't have Izabela's fingerprints because her body was too decomposed," he argued. "It's highly likely that that print was Izabela Lewicka's."

The prosecutor also attacked the defense's suggestion that Lisa Stasi might have abandoned her baby. "I think we all

Chapter 38

It was 2:55 P.M. Tuesday, October 29, 2002, when the jury foreman hit the buzzer to let the bailiff know they had reached a verdict. The six men and six women had deliberated for a total of eleven hours over two days, prompting speculation that they might be deadlocked on one of the counts or simply taking their time in considering the testimony of 110 witnesses and some five hundred pieces of evidence. Within twenty minutes, the prosecutors, defense lawyers and family members had reassembled in the courtroom for the long-anticipated moment of truth.

Linda Carter, the Victim Assistance Coordinator for the trial, caught Carolyn Trouten's eye as she and her ex-husband made their way down the aisle to the front row directly behind the prosecutor's table. "Are you okay?" Carter mouthed silently. Even with Harry by her side, Carolyn barely managed an unconvincing shrug in response to the question. She was so nervous. "Good luck," Carter mouthed again as Kathy Klinginsmith, Lisa Stasi's sister-in-law, and her mother-in-law, Betty Stasi, took seats next to the Troutens. Lisa's aunt Karen Moore was behind them.

Robinson's most ardent supporter throughout the trial, daughter Christy Shipps, sat on the opposite side of the crowded courtroom looking pale and apprehensive. She mouthed the words, "I love you" to her father as he was led in by two deputies, taking his customary place at the defense table between Billam and O'Brien. The deputies stood guard behind his chair and four more took up positions at the doors.

to those closely watching him that he was more upset about the sex toys conviction.

Unbelievable, Roth thought.

Several jurors would later confirm that they had never come close to being deadlocked on any of the charges. They were simply being careful, reviewing all the evidence for each of the six counts. "We spent a lot of time on each one," said Carl Macan, a retired pharmaceutical salesman who was known as Juror No. 184 for the duration of the trial. "We didn't rush through any of them. We decided we were not going to try and sell anybody if they didn't agree. But it was a slam dunk. Every vote we took in the guilt phase was twelve to nothing."

Back in the courtroom, O'Brien attempted to console Christy, who was quietly crying as she gathered her coat and purse. Across the aisle, tears of a different kind were streaming down the faces of Klinginsmith and Moore. Dave Brown went over and gave Carolyn a big hug. "At the risk of sounding sappy, I did get a little teary-eyed," the detective remembered. "I was so happy for Carolyn and her family and the families of the other victims."

Roth and Dougan exchanged looks of victory but kept it at that out of deference to Shipps, so distraught right in front of them. "It was the cap to the biggest case I would ever be involved with," Roth later said. "I was on cloud nine."

The sheriff's deputies standing just outside the courtroom door had been able to relay the verdicts to Reed and Wilson as soon as the judge read them aloud. "Finally justice was being served," said Reed, who felt vindicated.

"He had been such an arrogant jerk for so long," agreed Wilson. "I really believe he thought he would beat the charge [and] I found satisfaction in the fact that we finally got him!"

Members of the press corps gathered on the steps of the courthouse to await the families of the victims. Lisa Stasi's aunt Karen Moore was the first to emerge from the building. "It's just been a long time coming and we're very happy about the

gag order had not been lifted. With their reporting done for the day, the media rushed to computers to write their stories or broadcast live from in front of the courthouse.

Back in Virginia, Vickie had been checking her e-mail and Web sites carrying Kansas City news by the hour since arriving home. It was hard for her to sleep or think about anything else. She was furious about the judge's decision to throw out the aggravated sexual battery charge and believed, erroneously, that the detectives had tape-recorded her encounter with Robinson. "I know you do not want to hear from me," Greg Wilson e-mailed her upon returning to the office that afternoon, "but the jury just returned a 'guilty' on ALL charges and I thought you'd like to know."

Within minutes, she received similar messages from Linda Carter and *The Kansas City Star*'s Tony Rizzo. "I was ecstatic . . . and somewhat stunned," Vickie later said. "For the jury to be so open and so unanimous gave me back a faith or confidence that I had lost at trial. Also, the jury had read parts of my testimony during deliberation . . . or so I was told and the judge allowed it. I hoped that something—anything—I said during my testimony had made an impact. The 'biggest' thought I had, however, was 'Well, you lost the battle, but you won the war.' I had spoken for the victims and now their justice had been served. The verdict began the closure process."

The same jury that had just convicted Robinson of capital murder would reconvene in two days to begin the death penalty phase. The judge had said he didn't expect testimony to last more than a few days, leading several reporters to speculate that Robinson's fate would likely be sealed by the weekend.

Robinson would not pose a threat to anyone if given life in prison. "You don't have to kill John Robinson to incapacitate him," he said. "You can meet justice with compassion. One man or woman with courage can make a difference."

Nancy Robinson was the first witness called by the defense. For the first time in his four-week trial, Robinson showed his emotions as his wife, wearing a navy dress with a prim white collar, took the stand and testified about his eight-year-old granddaughter's visit to see him at the Johnson County Jail. The little girl was having some difficulties, Nancy said, and wanted very badly to see the grandfather who had taken care of her several times a week. "They have a bond that is unbelievable," she stated. "She is the apple of his eye."

Nancy explained that she and her daughter Christy Shipps waited in the lobby of the jail while a guard escorted her granddaughter to meet the defendant. Later, the little girl came back, Nancy said, and told how she had thrown her arms around her grandfather and, in reference to his prison garb, said: "Papa, orange is not your color."

Upon hearing her testimony, Robinson's shoulders shook and he took off his glasses and began wiping tears from his eyes with a handkerchief.

Nancy divulged several details in an effort to paint her husband as the devoted head of a tight-knit family: When Kim was about a year old, the little girl they called "Princess" had become very ill. They took her to the hospital, thinking she had a bad case of the flu. But doctors told them there was a problem with her brain and they wanted to perform exploratory surgery. "We talked about it and [my husband] said, 'We're not going to do that to her,'" she recalled, adding that they had to sign her out against medical advice. In the end, John had made the right decision. "In three days, she was acting like herself again."

She also described her husband as being very involved with their children as they were growing up. Kim and Christy played volleyball; John junior and Chris played soccer—and their proud father attended most if not all of their games. While John

the facts as you have, but they grew up with somebody else."
Asked how they felt about the possibility of his execution, she
dabbed at her eyes with Kleenex. "It's devastating, absolutely
devastating," she said, sobbing. "He's their dad; he's their
grandfather. They love him."

On cross-examination, however, prosecutor Paul Morrison
poked several holes in Nancy's portrayal of John Robinson.
He noted that she had testified for her husband when he was
convicted of fraud in 1986. "That didn't break the marital
bond, did it?" he asked.

Calling Robinson the "infidel deluxe," Morrison questioned
how Nancy could stand by him despite numerous affairs over
the years. "In fact, you're still married to him today," he said.
"Is *murder* enough to break the marital bond for you?"

"I don't know," she mumbled nervously. "Not right now."

Morrison also asked her why she didn't tell the police that
her husband had brought home a baby when they were investigating the disappearance of Lisa and Tiffany Stasi in 1985.
"I was not asked," she replied. "If you don't know what
they're looking for, you can't volunteer anything."

Morrison continued to hammer away. "Would it affect your
opinion if you knew that your husband had taken [your grand-
daughter] along on BDSM liaisons?" Morrison asked.
"Would *that* change your opinion?"

"Mr. Morrison!" cried Nancy, visibly agitated, as the defense objected.

But Morrison insisted he had evidence that Robinson had
indeed brought his granddaughter along on sadomasochistic
sex encounters, and if necessary, he was ready to present the
proof.

"I know this is stressful for you; however, it is not an argument," said Judge Anderson as he instructed the witness to
answer the question.

"I don't know," she replied, flustered.

Morrison also presented her with the note she had written
to her husband in November 1999—the same note detectives

with any regularity. His other three children—despite Nancy's testimony about how much they loved their father—had not been to the jail at all.

Standing before the yellow barrels that had served as coffins for Suzette and Izabela, Morrison began his closing remarks the next afternoon. In asking for the death penalty, he said the state was presenting only one aggravating circumstance—"and it's a big one," he added—the fact that Robinson had intentionally and with forethought killed five women and a teenage girl over a fifteen-year period.

He asked jurors to consider whether they had heard any facts or circumstances that reduced his moral culpability. "They're not there," he argued. "Words cannot describe the enormity of the crimes committed by the defendant [or] the enormity of the loss of the victims' families."

Citing testimony from the previous day, the prosecutor said Mark Cunningham had failed to find out if Robinson's bait of choice—a computer—would be available in prison. He said Robinson has always been a liar and con man and was unlikely to change his ways if allowed to live. "His way is manipulation. His way is deceit," he said. "And it often ends in tragic consequences."

Morrison also talked about Nancy Robinson, calling her a pathetic figure. "She takes the term 'stand by your man' to a whole new level," he said. "She is, in many ways, another victim of this man. Her life has probably been ruined because of what he has done to her and that family." And yet, as he noted, the family had begged the court to spare his life, claiming that his death would deprive them of his company. "It doesn't get any more audacious than that," he said. "Can you be a great dad when you're in prison? Can you be a great grandfather when you do the kinds of things he has done?"

Wrapping up the first half of his closing arguments by asking jurors to consider what's "fair and just," Morrison yielded the floor to Berrigan, who picked up on the same theme and spoke about how the jurors had been chosen for those very

move barrels containing women's bodies and mentioned a palm print and a fingerprint found on key pieces of evidence that did not belong to him.

In establishing guilt, Berrigan said it didn't matter whether there was evidence of another person's involvement because all accomplices are equally guilty of a crime. But if someone else were involved in the crimes, Robinson would be less deserving of a death sentence. "These questions should be answered before anybody's put to death," he said.

Morrison, reclaiming the floor for his rebuttal, said he had been struck by Berrigan's description of his client as non-threatening. "Look at him," he said as he pointed at Robinson. "Does he look like someone who would be into BDSM? Does he look like someone who would collect thousands and thousands of dollars in checks? Kill a nineteen-year-old woman for her baby? Stuff bodies into barrels? That's exactly why this man is so very, very dangerous."

Quoting from the Robert Duvall film, the district attorney said Robinson wanted the jury to grant him the "tender mercies" of life—small pleasures that included hearing rainfall on a roof or savoring a cup of fresh coffee in the morning. Yet, he said, Robinson had denied his six victims those same tender mercies. "They don't get to listen to the rain," he said. "They don't get to have a cup of coffee."

The defendant showed neither mercy nor remorse for his victims, Morrison continued. He didn't cry during testimony about the victims, he noted, but only when his wife talked about his granddaughter visiting him in jail. "He cried for himself," he thundered. "That says it all. He doesn't care about anybody but himself."

Concluding his remarks, Morrison said it was his belief that the death penalty should be reserved for only the most heinous of premeditated and intentional crimes. Rapping on the yellow barrels for emphasis, he paused and looked directly at the sixteen men and women sitting before him in the jury box. "If not him," he demanded, "who?"

the Bible for a fleeting instant but then forgot all about it as they returned to the jury room. Resuming their deliberations, they quickly took another vote. The tally this time was unanimous—12 to 0 for death. "We were getting ready to push the button, but the foreman asked if we would like to talk about our decision first," Mahan said.

They went around the table until they got to Juror No. 147— a big, burly man with dark hair and beard who had voted to impose the death penalty the night before. He picked up the Bible and cited several passages he had marked about mercy. "After I read this, I knew my decision was right," the juror allegedly said. No sooner had he done so than Judge Anderson strode into the jury room and asked, "Is there a Bible in here?"

When Juror No. 147 said he had one, "Judge Anderson's jaw about hit the floor," Macan recalled. The juror told the judge he had found the Bible in his hotel room. "It wasn't supposed to be there," the judge replied, escorting him from the room.

Over the next five hours, Judge Anderson and the lawyers individually questioned each juror privately about how or if the Bible was used. According to attorneys, during his night in sequestration, Juror No. 147 had read and jotted down several passages that stated that only God could grant mercy and only after a person had admitted wrongdoing and asked for forgiveness. He said the passages only confirmed that his decision to vote for death was correct.

At first, Mahan said she didn't think too much about the fact that the Bible had been brought into the jury room. "I figured it was like the newspapers or magazines we weren't supposed to have," she later said. "But as the day went on and the attorneys came and went from the judge's chambers, with my legal experience, I became extremely afraid of a mistrial. By the time the judge called us into the courtroom, I was physically sick to my stomach worrying about what was going to happen."

Rick Roth, who arrived at the courthouse that morning after hearing from Sara Welch that the jury had reached a verdict, realized there was something wrong when Sara walked into the

hoping and praying for. If there had to be a purpose to my little sister's life, it's that she stopped this man from hurting another soul." Kathy Klinginsmith, Lisa Stasi's sister-in-law, was relieved. "I'm just glad it's over," she said.

Other family members who couldn't be in the courtroom that day also praised the jury's recommendation. "That's what we wanted because that's what he deserves," Lisa Stasi's mother, Pat Sylvester, later reached by phone in Alabama, told *The Kansas City Star.* "I'm happy knowing he will never hurt anybody else." Beverly Bonner's former husband, William Bonner, in Arizona, said he believed Robinson was a sociopath who would never show any remorse for his crimes. "I think [the death penalty] is appropriate," he reportedly said.

"The weasel got what he deserves," Sheila Faith's sister, Michelle Fox, in Texas, agreed. "I think it's too easy, though, to just put him on a gurney and shoot him up with toxins."

That night, after the trial was finally over, Morrison attended a charity board dinner with his wife. It wasn't until then, he noted, that the trial, the verdict and the death sentence really sank in. "I was in the rest room still sort of shell-shocked that this thing was finally over," said the prosecutor, chuckling as he recalled the moment. "I looked in the mirror and I had these big bags under my eyes. And I thought, 'Gosh, I look like hell.'"

The death penalty verdict prompted Heather Tiffany Robinson to post her final thoughts to CourtTV.com's message board November 11. "You people really amaze me," she said in response to several readers who had written that they were glad that Robinson had been sentenced to death. "You're happy he has the death penalty? So by supporting his death, you are supporting killing. You teach your children: "Two wrongs don't make a right." [Killing him] will not bring back the victims. Hell, it won't give me back part of my childhood I lost and it won't help his family, either. The worst punishment would be

Heather Tiffany posted one final addendum, stressing that she was speaking only for herself. "My thoughts are my thoughts alone," she wrote. "They are spoken on my behalf and my behalf alone. Whatever I say comes from me, not my family or my friends."

A few weeks later, on December 9, 2002, the defense filed a massive 220-page challenge to their client's convictions, citing more than one hundred grounds for a new trial or an outright acquittal. The first issue on their list? The Bible brought into the courtroom on the last day of deliberations. They argued that Juror No. 147 had violated Robinson's right to a fair trial by using an outside source in making his decision. "As a general proposition, a defendant is entitled to a verdict based solely on the evidence and arguments presented in court and rendered in accordance with the court's instructions," the lawyers wrote.

The defense filing also attacked decisions and actions of the judge and prosecutors from the time detectives had begun investigating Robinson in March 2000 until final jury deliberations in early November 2002. Most of the issues had already been raised by the defense and ruled on by Judge Anderson before and during Robinson's trial.

Because the judge refused their request to move the trial, they argued that Robinson had been left with a jury biased by pretrial publicity. The defense also claimed that a lack of preparation time left them unable to effectively represent Robinson. "Counsel simply did not conduct an adequate investigation of Mr. Robinson's background, character and mental condition necessary for a constitutional trial on the issue of punishment," they wrote. They also objected to statements made by Morrison in closing arguments, saying he went beyond what was permissible under the law.

Prosecutors responded only to the new defense arguments. The juror who took his Bible with him into deliberations did not commit misconduct, they argued several weeks later. The jurors already had taken their final vote before there was any conversation about Bible passages. Kansas law prohibits

Chapter 41

Rejecting all defense motions for acquittal on Tuesday, January 21, 2003, Judge Anderson gave John Robinson one last opportunity to bare his soul, asking the convicted murderer if he had anything he wished to present before learning his fate. The defendant, however, rose briefly to his feet and declined. "I have nothing," replied Robinson, sharply dressed, as always, in a gray suit with a pale blue tie. While he chose silence, his daughter stood at a podium placed in front of the gallery and pleaded with the judge on behalf "of all the children and grandchildren" to spare her father's life. "Your Honor, you are in a position to both dispense justice and mercy at the same time," said Christy Shipps, who, with her mother, attended the final proceedings on the bitterly cold morning.

Robinson's most loyal supporter tearfully described her father's prosecution as an "emotional roller coaster" that had strained the familial bonds to their maximum limit. She said they had to accept things they would never understand, but she emphasized that the horrible things heard in court did not reflect the loving man who had taught them to put family first and to respect the law. "The John Robinson we know has always been a loving and supportive father and grandfather," said Christy, wearing a red turtleneck and black pants.

The paramedic described how her eight-year-old daughter had been deeply affected by being separated from the grandfather she used to see almost every day. "Every day she asks God for one little hug from her Papa," she said, sobbing. She asked the judge to think of Robinson's seven grandchildren.

her sister-in-law—Lisa's mother, Pat Sylvester—counted themselves fortunate to have gotten to know her in the 2.5 years since they learned she was alive. "But Heather had a right to be with her mother," Moore argued emotionally. "She had the right to know her uncle Marty and her grand-mother, and her great grandmother, and her great, great grandmother, and all the rest of the family. My sister-in-law lost both of her children [Lisa and Marty] because of John Robinson, because when he killed Lisa, he killed Marty as well. And he put our family through hell on earth for eighteen years. John Robinson has shown no regard for human life, no regard for the highest laws of the land, and I have never seen one ounce of remorse on his face. He should receive that which he brought upon himself—the penalty of capital punishment."

Carolyn Trouten and Suzette's sister Kim Padilla, who had driven with several family members through a blinding snow-storm to get to Kansas for the judge's sentencing, also made passionate pleas. Carolyn said she didn't view death as a pun-ishment for Robinson or revenge for her daughter's murder but merely as insurance that he would never be able to kill again. "He took my little girl and I am never going to quit missing her," she said, tears streaming down her face.

"John Robinson lured Suzette with promises of a better life and he took that life away," added an equally emotional Kim, who bore a strong resemblance to her murdered sister.

Mother and daughter both took issue with what Christy Shipps had told the judge. "[We] don't have the opportunity to beg for Suzette's life," Padilla said bitterly. Carolyn ques-tioned why Robinson's family would even want their children to be around him. "Seems to me if they had any sense, they'd want him to be executed, too," she told the judge.

Paul Morrison followed the women to the podium and said he felt an obligation to speak for the family of Izabela Lewicka, who lived in Indiana and could not bear the thought of ever again setting foot in Kansas. He recalled the recent

maximum term provided by law," he said before lifting the judicial gag order that had been in place since Robinson's arrest.

There to witness the judge's sentence were several of the investigators who had worked so hard to bring Robinson to justice, including Rick Roth and Stephen Haymes, who had played such critical roles at the beginning and end of Robinson's decades-long murder career. Both men said they felt a measure of relief and closure that the defendant had at long last gotten what he deserved. Carl Macan and Debbie Mahan, who attended along with four of the other jurors, felt the same way.

Macan, mincing no words, said his reaction to the verdict was "Death cannot come fast enough for him—like give him the needle tomorrow morning." Mahan, more circumspect, agreed that he deserved to die, but she also noted that she could understand why Christy Shipps had pleaded for her father's life. However, she, too, questioned why she would want her daughter exposed to such a monster. "If he killed one woman instead of six, it might have made a difference," she said, "but his life certainly is not worth more than the six lives he took. What really sealed it was when he had a chance to speak and chose not to—maybe because he still [had] to stand trial in Missouri?"

Lisa Stasi's aunt and Suzette Trouten's mother, aunt, grandmother and two sisters gathered after the sentencing for an impromptu press conference in the district attorney's library on the fifth floor. It had been an emotional day and many of the women's eyes were red from crying as they squeezed around the rectangular table. Carolyn Trouten was still outwardly seething, not only at Christy for pleading with the judge to spare her father's life but also at Nancy for turning a blind eye to her husband's criminal behavior. "I am almost as mad at them [the Robinson family] as I am at him," she said. "I think his wife could have stopped all this. If she would have just done something, anything, when he brought that baby home in 1985, then all our girls wouldn't be dead now."

Carolyn and her daughters reiterated their belief—one that had been verbalized by many others—that Robinson finally

Paul Morrison and Sara Welch also spoke publicly to reporters about the case for the first time since the gag order had been imposed shortly after Robinson's arrest. The prosecutor told the group that one of the first things he tries to do when he meets the families of victims is to explain he can't make things the way they were. "We can't make their lives whole again," he said. "We can't reverse the clock. What we hope to be able to do for victims of crime is to let them walk away feeling like they got some measure of justice."

His office had put in thousands of hours on the case and Morrison joked that in recent months he had spent more time with Welch than he had with his wife. Even then, two people were barely enough to get their arms around and make sense of all the evidence, he said. They had taken off a few days in spring 2002 because they knew they'd be working long hours, seven days a week, all summer and during the trial. Often the seamy nature of Robinson's activities made the prosecutors feel like clerks in a sex shop, he noted, and they had only slowly become conditioned to the graphic nature of BDSM.

One of their biggest challenges, Morrison also said, was to make the enormously complicated case understandable to a jury. It was very gratifying when they talked to jurors after the verdict and were told that the trial was much like watching a movie. "They said they didn't have much trouble following it," he said. "They would come in each day and watch the next chapter unfold. Which is what we wanted."

There were hugs between Linda Carter, Terri Issa and Shirley Fessler from the DA's staff and the Trouten women as the press conference came to an end and everyone got up to leave.

Karen Moore quietly asked Linda if she could use her phone to call her sister-in-law and tell her the good news. Pat Sylvester, she confided, had suffered two heart attacks since Robinson's arrest and had not been well enough to attend. She was at home in Alabama, though, hoping and praying for the death penalty. "We are both very strong Christians and a lot

Epilogue

On January 24, 2003, three days after Judge Anderson sentenced him to death, Robinson was quietly transferred from the Johnson County Jail, where he'd lived since his arrest, to a small solitary cell at the El Dorado Correctional Facility outside Wichita, the destination for men facing capital punishment in Kansas. There he joined six others waiting to die—including the notorious Carr brothers, recently convicted of raping and robbing four young adults before executing them in a snow-covered soccer field—and received the first taste of the maximum-security prison that will more than likely serve as his final home.

For two months, Robinson lived in the Administrative Segregation Unit, separated from other inmates, and was allowed outside for a maximum of one hour a day, five days a week, but only to shower or exercise. If he exercised at all, he did it alone in an enclosed area, where he could shoot baskets, walk around and stretch, but not lift weights. He received three meals a day, passed through a slot in a solid metal door. Through the "Bean Hole," too, he could talk to his death row inmates, though technically the prison does not allow such conversations. His cell, measuring 8' x 10', was comprised of concrete floors and walls, a metal combination toilet and sink, a bed mounted to a wall, a writing table and narrow windows with hardened glass. In order to earn the privilege of having a radio or television, he would have to follow every prison rule for 120 days. He also would have to demonstrate good behavior before he could receive visitors, and even then he would remain behind glass and tightly shackled.

souri had executed sixty people since reinstating capital punishment in 1975. Kansas hadn't executed anyone since 1965 and only reinstated the death penalty in 1994. Robinson couldn't be blamed for thinking he just might cop a plea and beat the death penalty in Missouri and take his chances that his sentence would be overturned on appeal in Kansas.

Several people doubted that Koster could get Robinson to reveal any useful information for a plea bargain. Robinson's former attorneys had approached Morrison and Welch just before the Kansas trial to talk about a similar type of arrangement and they had politely refused in part because they didn't trust a word he said. Some of those in law enforcement also held the belief that Robinson had long ago disposed of the women's bodies in a Kansas City location now covered by concrete. Even if he admitted that was where the women could be found, they'd face a troubling dilemma. "It would be just like the arrogant son of a bitch to send us on a wild-goose chase, spending all kinds of money digging up this [site] for nothing," said one source. "I can just see him sitting back and laughing his ass off."

Some of the missing women's relatives had decided, in any case, they didn't want to learn how their loved ones had died. Karen Moore, Lisa Stasi's aunt, was one of them. "Just speaking for me, I don't know that I want to know," she said moments after the judge had sentenced him to death. "I think there is a little bit of peace in not knowing."

Paula Godfrey's father, Bill, wasn't holding his breath for a confession and appeared confident that the death sentence in Kansas would stand. "He's already facing the death penalty," he reportedly said. "There isn't much more they can do to him, which is a shame."

At the same time, the relatives and friends of Bonner and the Faiths were pushing hard for a trial in Missouri. It wasn't enough that Johnson County jurors had contemplated evidence about their loved ones before they convicted Robinson and sentenced him to death for the murders of the three women in Kansas. They wanted convictions, too. "To remember Sheila

Under either scenario, Robinson will be an old man, probably close to seventy, by the time he exhausts his appeals. Assuming that Kansas finishes first, Robinson would be moved from El Dorado to the Lansing Correctional Facility, outside of Kansas City, the week of his death. There, on the fourth floor of a century-old stone building, he would spend his last few days in a one-of-a-kind cell less than a dozen paces from the small starkly white room where he would die.

On the appointed morning, Robinson would be allowed a last meal prepared by the prison or $15 worth of food from a Lansing restaurant. If he so chose, he would have an approved spiritual adviser visit him before the execution and be with him in the death chamber. Shortly beforehand, the warden would read the court order of execution, which would be carried out at 11:00 A.M. A six-person team would escort Robinson from his cell down a short hall to the death chamber.

Once inside, the tie-down team would fasten leather restraints around his wrists and ankles. Two medically trained corrections officers would insert intravenous catheters—one of them a backup—to each arm. As many as thirteen witnesses would be escorted into one of three rooms. Three of those witnesses would be of his own choosing and they would sit behind smoked windows, where he could see them and they him. The other witnesses, including victims' relatives, government officials and reporters, would be in two other rooms hidden behind mirrored windows.

Then, the warden would pull back a curtain from the three windows and call the secretary of corrections, who would in turn verify with the Kansas attorney general and governor that there was no legal reason to stop the proceedings. Upon the warden's order, the IV team would push a button to administer the lethal cocktail of drugs, which would travel from an adjoining room through a hole in the wall into his arms. Sodium Pentothal would put Robinson to sleep, followed by pancreozymin bromide to stop his breathing. Finally potassium chloride would stop his heart.

in a small chapel in Tennessee, they were married. Sadly, however, her story book romance did not have a Cinderella ending. Within a few months the relationship had soured and, as of this writing, Vickie was headed for divorce.

"It's sad because I feel lost," Vickie wrote in a recent e-mail. "I feel like Dorothy and want to hold my little dog in a basket close to my heart, click my silver heels, close my eyes and repeat, 'There's no place like home.' The problem is, when I close my eyes, I cannot envision home. I'm unsettled—not grounded. Lol! And Kansas is definitely NOT home."

She said she could not over-emphasize the connection she felt with Robinson's victims. "They felt like sisters to me— even though I had not met any of them and [they] were of different alternative lifestyles and different from myself," she said. "But I felt this bond like nothing I've ever experienced before. I knew it could have been me that had fallen silent."

Despite her experiences, Vickie still believed the Internet was a wonderful creation. "It puts us in touch with the world," she said. "We have to be wise, however, and alert to signals and red flags that might caution us of potential danger. Robinson was nothing more than a serial killer who made his way online to find more victims. In my opinion, it was never about sex, of any style. It was about pretending to be someone the women desired him to be, then from there finding his way to the path that gave him a great sense of power and satisfaction, finding the way to brutally kill women who trusted him. It was his life's work and he had become very good at it. One can't blame the Internet or meeting online for his actions."

For the time being, however, Vickie had no plans and no desire to date anyone—online or otherwise. "I've got to find some more inner strength to make it on my own," she said. "For once in my life, I am reaching out to others, not [only] online, but in real life. My love is greatest for my children and always has been. Then, of course, Mary Kate has given unconditional love through it all!"

She said her next move would be to relocate to an undis-

would imagine their hard-nosed, rough-edged sergeant used to spend his Sunday morning teaching third graders. [He's also a] great Dad. Doting Grandpa. Generous to a fault. I am so lucky to have him."

Welch was happy to report that wedding plans were nearly complete. "We have a church, reception site, caterer and DJ," she said. "Bridesmaid dresses are bought. Now I need to get my dress. What is Roth's contribution to the planning and coordination of this event you ask? Zero. Oh well, I should thank my lucky stars he is not involved. His idea of a reception menu is beanie weenies, BBQ potato chips and beer. But I bet he will look pretty dapper in his tux, which is all that matters."

Author's note: On October 16, 2003, as this book was going to press, John Robinson walked into a Cass County courtroom and pleaded guilty to murdering not only Beverly Bonner, Sheila and Debbie Faith, but also Paula Godfrey and Catherine Clampitt. One of his attorneys said his motivations were to avoid a possible death sentence in Missouri and save his family the embarrassment of another trial. When embarking last winter on plea negotiations, DA Chris Koster explained that he hoped to convince Robinson to lead authorities to the bodies of Godfrey, Clampitt and Stasi. But after the October hearing, he told reporters he had become convinced that the women's remains had been "disposed of in a way that were not recoverable."

Johnson County DA Paul Morrison said he was glad of the closure for the families involved. But he called the plea agreement in Missouri "classic John Robinson" and stated that the defendant, whose word could not be trusted, had once again taken advantage of the system. The district attorney added that Robinson would soon be returned to the El Dorado Correctional Facility outside Wichita to await the appeals court ruling on his Kansas death sentence.

primarily white, which supports the data that most serial crimes are primarily intra-racial. His victims, with the exception of 15-year-old Debbie Faith, were between the ages of eighteen and fifty, also in keeping with the average age of serial murder victims. In a study I did of 107 American serial killers, I found that only 3 percent of offenders murdered younger teens.

Robinson, moreover, is similar to other serial killers in terms of the number of his victims. He has been convicted of killing three women—Lisa Stasi, Izabela Lewicka and Suzette Trouten—and on October 16, 2003, he agreed to plead guilty to the murders of five other women he had been suspected of killing—Paula Godfrey, Catherine Clampitt, Beverly Bonner and Sheila and Debbie Faith—in order to avoid a possible death sentence in Missouri. That puts his total number of victims at eight. Likewise, serial killers in the United States have an average of eight known victims.

However, a different picture emerges when Robinson's age is compared to that of other serial murderers. He was fifty-six when he was arrested and subsequently charged with murder in June 2000. In my study, I found that the average age of serial killers at the time of their arrest was thirty. Only 18 percent, in fact, were over the age of forty-two. Clearly, Robinson was older than the typical serial killer when he was arrested. The question is whether he was older than the typical serial killer when he started to murder women.

In my opinion, Robinson's first victim probably wasn't Paula Godfrey. In 1984, when she went missing, he would have been forty years of age, which is old to start a career as a serial murderer. There's a good chance that Robinson murdered women we don't know about dating back as far as the 1970s. There is also a sizeable gap in time between the alleged murders of Bonner and the Faiths in 1994 and Lewicka in 1999. Considering that three of his victims (Godfrey, Clampitt and Stasi) have not been found, it would not surprise me to learn that he had managed to hide the remains of other women.

What were the motives behind his extreme measures? Robinson was the ultimate con man. He lived his entire adult life creating business scams in order to defraud people out of their hard earned money. Each successful scam undoubtedly gave him a psychological rush—not so much because of the currency he pocketed but because he had outsmarted someone. Soon, however, he found he needed to pull off more and bigger cons to experience the same euphoria. He may have started out by stealing postage stamps but he soon graduated to conning and murdering women.

Robinson clearly profited financially from at least four of the victims. This was certainly true of Bonner and the Faiths. Killing Lisa Stasi and arranging the fraudulent adoption of her daughter to his unsuspecting brother not only made him money but also made him feel important. While his motives for the murders of Lewicka and Trouten are less obvious, the evidence suggests that these women had become a burden. His wife was asking questions about Lewicka and a second girlfriend, Barbara Sandre, was moving into town. In Trouten's case, he had promised to take her to California and Hawaii. but how was he going to do that and keep up the charade at home? We know even less about Robinson's motives when it comes to his involvement with Godfrey and Clampitt. It is not unusual, however, for a killer to exhibit similar behavior in his murders but have different underlying motives for that behavior.

One of the questions that was raised in this case was whether Robinson is a sexual sadist. Richard von Kraft-Ebing coined the term after the Marquis de Sade, whose writings describe a pairing of sexual acts with domination, degradation, and violence. A majority of sexual sadists never engage in sexually sadistic acts, much less a crime. Among those who choose to act on their fantasies, there are many who limit their actions to lawful behaviors with consenting or paid partners.

The Diagnostic and Statistical Manual of Mental Disorders (DSM-IV) definition for sexual sadism is often used to classify

- Other people should recognize how special I am.
- No one's needs should interfere with my own.

   Historically, serial killers have experienced intense family conflicts during childhood that fuel their distrust towards the world quite early in life and cause them to turn inward and become self-absorbed. Information about Robinson's childhood is sketchy at best and it is unlikely that a full account will ever come to light, especially since his parents are no longer living. His son reportedly told police that Robinson claimed to have been physically and emotionally abused by his mother. However, Robinson himself has given conflicting accounts to prison psychiatrists over the years, hinting in one that his childhood was ideal while in another that his mother had been a strict disciplinarian who lacked intimacy.

   In September 2002, on the eve of the trial, Robinson's lawyers hired Dr. Dorothy Lewis to conduct a new psychological evaluation. She interviewed Robinson twice, spoke with some members of his family and reviewed incomplete documentation currently available on his mental and medical history. She reported that he had a history of severe physical and emotional abuse throughout childhood, resulting in episodic dissociative states. She also discovered that as many as four generations of family members may have suffered from psychiatric illness and that Robinson may have a bipolar mood disorder, although she said substantial additional testing was needed to reach a final conclusion. All further details of her investigation, however, were filed under court seal at the request of the defendant.

   Interviews with other serial killers, however, have revealed a hatred of women for wrongs they believe have been done to them in the past. It is possible that Robinson experienced traumatic rejection from his mother or former girlfriends or women he fantasized about. Whether these wrongs were fact or fiction is not the issue; what matters is that Robinson's feelings of hate, anger and rage were undeniably real. In cases

son's desire for financial gain and to satisfy his psychological need for power and control. His attitude toward and treatment of his victims manifested itself in the form of seeing the women as merely objects, a 'prop' to use and abuse as he saw fit. He viewed these women as nothing more than a 'means to an end.' In the end, though, Robinson was a master of nothing but the plight of his life—death.